The Truth About Me

ISBN 0-9704618-0-1
All rights reserved
Copyright Mentor International Inc.
(Standard Copyright License)
Second Edition
(First Edition published under title The Angel Within Me ©2000)
Published by Mentor International Inc. 2012

This book is dedicated to the strongest woman I know, my mom!

The Truth About Me

These secrets I'm keeping nobody knows
The depths of my struggles are locked in my soul
I'd give you the key and I'd let you come in
But I know I can't trust you, there's no one I can
I've trusted before and I've seen where that's led
Pictures are painted then tear drops are shed
So I'll go it alone so safely I'll be
No one quite knowing the truth about me
The truth about me, I want to be free
Free from these fears that I carry with me
Maybe it's time that the truth guides my way
You're only as sick as your secrets they say
I'd finish this song if I knew how it goes
Not much to say when the truth is untold
God send me an angel a friend that I know
I promise I'll share from the depths of my soul
These secrets I've buried inside for so long
Then I'll pick up my pen and I'll finish this song

Rachelle Rose

One

I was raised to believe a lie. A lie about myself, life, God, and the world. The funny thing is they called it The Truth. "The Truth will set you free," they said, yet I felt imprisoned. I was raised by Jehovah's Witnesses. I knew nothing else. In early adolescence I began to question all of the false teachings they taught. I ran away from home and spent many confusing years in trauma. Through it all, I battled an invisible illness which no one knew about. After years of questioning all the lies I had been taught, I realized they were right about one thing; the truth did finally set me free. Only it was not the truth they talked of. It was my truth.

I knew at a young age what I wanted to do with my life. I was going to be a poet like Dr. Seuss. When I first laid eyes on his books, I knew I wanted to be just like him. I had never experienced anything that grabbed me quite the way his books did. It seems funny to think of it now, but I thought he had to be the most creative person there was.

When I was in first grade, I went through a huge transition. It was then that I began to feel like I was big. That meant I could read all by myself and that made me proud. But being big was also a little scary for me. I found that having to get up and go to school every day was very hard. Before, when I was still little, I woke up when I felt ready and could pretty much lie around and watch television or play all day. I missed that part of being little. Now there were responsibilities, I was expected to do so much now. I began feeling tired most of the time.

By the time I was in second grade, being big was no longer fun for me. Every morning when my mother woke me for school, I would just dread getting out of bed. As soon as I would stand up, the back of my neck and head would start hurting. I always took a hot shower in the morning and this seemed to help a little. But it would still hurt too much to be able to eat breakfast. Once I was at school, my headache was usually gone but then the grumbly tummy would start. All I could think about by mid-morning was getting to lunch. After lunch, I would feel better for a while, but then I would start getting sleepy. My head felt too heavy to hold up, and my legs were heavy and tired also. I wondered how all of the other kids could stand it. They never complained about being tired. Sometimes I wondered if I was the only one who felt like this.

I was raised as a Jehovah's Witness. My father was an Elder of our congregation. This made me stand out like a sore thumb in school. Life in the *Truth* as they called it was not easy. The *Truth*, is a term that Jehovah's Witness' use to describe their organization. Kids in school teased me for being weird and asked many questions that I was ashamed to answer. Being ashamed of my religion also made me feel horrible. I knew Jehovah God looked down on me for not wanting to spread his word and for being embarrassed of him. I knew my bad thoughts would probably cause me to die in the *Tribulation*, or even worse, maybe Satan and his demons would get me. Maybe they would see my lack of faith and possess me. Like the stories I heard of other congregation members being shaken in their beds and choked by the demons because they opened themselves to him through unclean acts. Despite my fear of God's wrath, I still could not shake my humiliation of being so different from the rest of my classmates. And I certainly did not have the heart to tell them they were all going to die in the tribulation because they were *worldly*, that is the term used for anyone who was not a Witness.

The Jehovah's Witness organization taught me that we were in a *universal war* that all people are inevitably caught up in, namely, that Satan had declared war on Jehovah, and we were automatically on one side or the other. If you were not doing all that the organization asked, you were on the side of the devil. I lived in fear of this because we were also told the Tribulation was coming soon and we would be destroyed if we did not live according to their laws. As a Witness child I was told to avoid *worldly* magazines, movies, TV shows, music, etc.

Any information not coming from the Witnesses was evil and dangerous and could cause Satan to come into my life. I lived in fear of Satan and had frequent nightmares about him. I was taught that even saying the pledge of allegiance could cause demonic control. I felt so awful that all the other kids in my class did not know this and were in so much danger. Yet at the same time I knew from past experience that trying to warn them would cause them to laugh at me and not want to be my friend. They already thought I was weird so I kept quiet.

Another thing I hated about being a Witness is how often we attended *meetings.* That is what they called their church services. We went on Sundays for two hours and on Tuesday and Thursday evenings. The sermons, or talks as they called them, were long and boring. We had to pay attention though because often we were quizzed after meetings.

Holidays were the worst. We didn't celebrate any holidays since Witnesses believed they were all Pagan customs and therefore unclean in Jehovah's eyes. No birthdays or Christmas, not even Easter.

When I went back to school after Christmas break, all of the other kids in my class had new clothes and talked of all the presents they had received for Christmas. This made me feel so unworthy and sad. When I was asked what I had got for Christmas I was supposed to recite the lines I had rehearsed so many times before. The Witnesses said this was a perfect opportunity to spread *the Truth* to others. But instead of spreading Gods word I would just say I don't celebrate. This always gave way to a look of disbelief and further questions, "Why don't you celebrate Christmas...Does it make you feel bad...You don't get even one present?" I hated this. I would wish I could disappear. I pretended I didn't care as I fought the lump in my throat. And always, after feeling sorry for myself came the awful guilt in my head, how dare I feel the way I did. I thought I was bad for this but I could not make myself get rid of the selfish thoughts.

Since my father was an Elder of our congregation, which is like a Pastor, our family had to be a good example for the congregation. Because of this my dad had to be extra strict with us. If we did not listen to him or my mother, or did anything wrong, we had to be punished because the bible says, "If you spare the rod, you will spoil the child." We definitely could not be spoiled with my dad's status in the congregation. This supposedly could have a terrible ripple effect on many people. So my dad set the example by giving us strict discipline.

Usually if we got in trouble, like talked back or didn't listen right away, we would be told to go to our rooms, pull down our pants, lean over the bed, and wait for dad to come and spank us. The wait always seemed so long. When my dad spanked, it was going to sting for a long time afterward, so waiting was truly torture. After our punishment came the shameful lecture of his and Jehovah's disappointment in us. This is what proved to leave the worst scar of all, the shame.

When I was about eight or nine, some weird things that I did not understand were happening with my parents. My mother began to cry a lot. She always cried in her room with the door locked. I always wanted to comfort her but I knew it would not be well received. In times past I had learned my lesson about that. If I tried to hug my mom when she was sad, she would get real stiff and push me away. She did not like affection and it felt like a big huge rock falling in my stomach when she pushed me away. It hurt deep inside me and as much as I yearned to comfort her, I could not risk feeling the sting of her rejection. So instead I would just listen to her cry, sometimes I would stand right outside her bedroom door, trying to convince myself to knock, the panic welling up in me to help her. But I would somehow shut it off and pretend it wasn't real. That was all I could do.

My parent's problems were very confusing to me. I did not understand what my mother was so sad about until one day, one of my mother's friends, Nancy, came to our doorstep very upset at my dad. She was calling him a liar and then punched him in his mouth before she left in hysterics. He came in with his lip bleeding and us girls were sent upstairs to our room. We did not dare to ask questions about this incident which was fine because I really did not want to know. Nancy was in our congregation and soon everyone knew about what had happened.

Nancy's daughter and I had been good friends up until this. After the incident we were not allowed to talk to each other. Soon after this, we had to switch to a different Kingdom Hall. So after years of becoming close to all the people in our congregation, we had to start over. This was so hard and painful because as a witness you are not allowed to associate with people outside of your faith and our congregation was our whole support, the only friends I'd ever known.

My dad stepped down as an Elder soon after this but he was still strict. My mom seemed like she was never there. She was physically there but not mentally. I felt such sadness in her and it was painful to helplessly watch her get worse. I did not understand what was going on. One day after school, my sisters and I came home to my dad, which was odd since he was always at work when we got home. He told us our mother was in the hospital and was very sick. He did not know when she would come home or even tell us what was wrong. He did however tell us she did not want to see us. That drove me crazy. I wanted to go to her and help her. I somehow knew her sickness was her sadness. I overheard talk of her taking too many pills. It seemed like forever before we got to see her. The house was dead without her and I was so excited to go to the hospital and run and hug her so she knew how much I wanted her. But when we got to the hospital and I saw her, I froze. I could hardly even talk to her. We were all uncomfortably silent and mom had her legs crossed and was jiggling them nervously. I had never seen her look so distant and emotionless.

During all of this, deep shame grew wildly inside of me. There had been an incident just prior to Nancy punching my dad that fed my quilt incredibly. Nancy's daughter and I had been playing together alone one day when we decided to explore each other's bodies. We were caught and our families reacted in utter shame over this. I distinctly remember the day my dad made the whole family sit at the kitchen table and I had to tell all of them exactly what I had done. I was so humiliated that I tried to make myself disappear by thinking really hard about it but there I sat in front of all of them. I could see the discomfort in my older sister, Shelly. She would never have done anything so awful. I knew she must have been so ashamed of me.

After this came out in the open, I never wanted to talk to anyone. I was sure everyone knew how bad I was. I was so embarrassed of myself and said a lot of mean punishing things to myself in my head. "You're bad, you're bad, Jehovah is ashamed of you, your family is ashamed of you, you don't deserve anything good." These kinds of thoughts played in my head over and over. I tried to punish myself for my bad deeds in order to get rid of the guilt, but the guilt just grew no matter how much pain I tried to inflict upon myself. I even tried to hurt myself by digging my nails into my skin, but still the guilt lingered. I knew I was destined to suffer Satan's wrath if I did not have true repentance but I did not know how much suffering I had to suffer to gain true repentance. Eventually, I learned to shut off my mind when the pain and fear I felt inside became unbearable. I had to shut down so I could face people. I always wondered how much of what I had done with Nancy's daughter had played a part in the terrible thing my parents were going through.

This was not the only bad thing I had done. I seemed to cause my parents a lot of trouble. That is why they called me the rebellious one.

I just wanted to have fun but it always seemed that I was in trouble. I would get really mad at them for things that I thought were unfair. I tried so hard to hold in my anger but sometimes the angry words would escape from me and I would have to be punished for talking back. This was most of my problem, expressing how I felt, but I learned over the years that how I felt was wrong and should not be expressed. I was taught, *the Truth will set you free,* the Truth being the Jehovah's Witness organization, but I could not seem to follow their rules. There was no hope for me.

At some point, I began feeling guilt over my thoughts and feelings, even when I managed not to say it out loud. It had been pounded in my head that Jehovah knew my thoughts and I could not escape him. I could not figure out how to be good, it seemed like I could not control the thoughts in my mind. Like wanting to play with worldly kids in my neighborhood or wishing to celebrate holidays. Soon I gave up trying to stop the awful wishes in my mind. I realized that I was just born bad and there was no hope for me.

By the time I was in fifth grade, I hated school, and debated whether I even liked life very much. It seemed to me that life was too hard most of the time. It never occurred to me that I shouldn't be feeling this way. As a child you do not really know what it is to feel normal. I had been having my guilt problems for such a long time. The headaches and fatigue that plagued me every day also became normal for me. I assumed there was something wrong with me for not being able to handle it. I felt as if I was different from all of the other kids. They seemed to be able to handle life just fine. I wanted to be like the other kids my age, but I had too many worries. I remember lying in bed at night trying to fall asleep. I'd be so upset about having to go to school and suffer through another painfully long day that I'd look at my clock and count the hours before I had to wake up. I tried to comfort myself by thinking of how long I had before morning came. By the time I fell asleep, usually there was not much time left before I had to get up for school.

I did not share these feelings with anyone. I was sure they would not believe me or think I wanted attention. I had often been told to quit feeling sorry for myself so I knew complaining would only bring more guilt. The morning headaches had been going on for so long that they seemed routine. Those I kept to myself also. I did not want my parents to be any more disappointed in me. I did not want them to know I wasn't like everyone else. I was sure

I was different and not as good as everyone else was. I thought I was just a bad seed.

I also had ear infections a lot. This had been a problem since I was very little. I think a lot of how I felt was blamed on my ears. When I was twelve I had surgery to repair my eardrum which was damaged due to the chronic infections. The surgery did relieve some of the pain, but I still felt tired often.

In the sixth grade, there was a boy in my class who started picking on me. He would call me flat face every day, all day. He whispered it every time he passed me. His friends and many of the other kids would laugh each time he did this to me. I was so incredibly embarrassed. After school I would go home and look in the mirror to check my face to see why he kept saying this. After this had gone on for a while I began to hate my face. When I would look in the mirror I hated the image looking back at me. I became very angry at this image and often would cry and say mean things to myself as I looked in the mirror. I would say things like, "I hate you. You are so ugly that no one wants to be your friend." I grew out my bangs and wore my hair in my face to try and hide. This went on for two years and the damage to my self-esteem was a deep and painful wound.

In seventh grade there was an incident with another group of boys in the same school that traumatized me further. One afternoon after lunch the three boys trapped me in the janitor's closet and sexually assaulted me. Then they spread terrible rumors about me. Even my friends would have nothing to do with me after this for fear they would be a target of these bullies. I had to switch to a new school because the torment was too awful to bear.

During my middle school years I had a lot of problems. I became very depressed. I did not want to do anything but sleep. I cried a lot during this period and felt so miserable. The headaches in the morning made me dread facing my day and the fatigue was becoming unbearable. I did not want to talk to the other kids in the new school because I was ashamed of who I was. I felt very alone. Dealing with these feelings was extremely difficult but I did not know what to do. I was so confused, and did not understand why I was so tormented. I often wondered if it was it my punishment from God.

I became bulimic during this period. It gave me a feeling of relief to make myself throw up. After I would eat, I would usually purge. I became terrified I would get fat and add to my ugliness. Soon just the feeling of being full from eating a meal sent me into a panic. I never told a soul about my bulimia.

Thank god for my best friend, Kim. Our mothers had been good friends since we were little and we grew very close during our middle school years. She kept me going. Spending time with her seemed to be the only thing in life I enjoyed anymore.

In the back of my mind, I still had dreams of being a poet. I also loved writing stories. I felt like I was good at it and this rare feeling of pride felt so good to me. Writing became my way of expressing myself during these confusing times. It helped me to sort out my feelings, even if I was writing something totally irrelevant to my life. It was a like a release for me to put my words on paper. Sometimes I would wake up during the night with a poem in my mind. It was as if the words were not coming from me rather put in my head. So I would jot it down and go back to sleep. Then in the morning I would go back over it and edit the poem. I didn't understand where this came from but it seemed to be messages for me so I had a trust in it. I began to feel it was angels or something helping me along.

When I started ninth grade, I went further downhill emotionally. I felt so bad about myself and could not muster the energy to deal with life. I secretly began skipping school. I would go on the bus to school but I never went in, I turned right around and walked home. My mother was gone to work by the time I got there and I would go back to bed for the rest of the day. I felt safe there. I had become so afraid to face the world. I just wanted to hide away forever.

One day while walking home in the morning after skipping school, a man in about his late twenties approached me. He started asking me questions, which made me very nervous. Finally I confessed to him that I was skipping school. His reaction shocked me. He was very understanding and sympathetic, like he knew my pain. I felt so relieved that someone was actually talking to me and caring about what I was going through. I opened up to him about some of my troubles with my parents. He walked with me and seemed to understand everything I told him, he even felt bad for me. This felt so good to me, no one ever acted so concerned and interested in me the way he did. I still felt a little nervous since he was a stranger plus a *worldly* man, but no matter what my mind told me I could not resist talking with him. Pretty soon we approached my block and I told him I had to go home. He invited me to his apartment, which he said was just a few blocks further. I knew I should not go with him, I knew how awful the punishment would be if I did but I could not resist the attention he was giving me felt so good.

When we reached his apartment he told me his name and talked a little bit about his life, which seemed to have a lot in common with mine. This eased my mistrust a little. When we walked into his place, I instantly got lightheaded and felt very scared. He put on some music, took off his shirt, and asked me to rub his back. I did not want to but I didn't want him to know how scared I was so I did. He asked me why my hands were shaking and I was completely embarrassed. I said I was cold and he laughed. Then he reached around and began rubbing my arm in a way that I knew was not good. He pulled me in to kiss me and I pushed away and said I had to go. I was fighting tears and my stomach ached with nervousness. I had a frantic feeling inside which got worse when he grabbed onto my hands and told me to stay. My face was hot and my mind was racing, frantically thinking of how to get out of there. What if he was going to kill me? What if he never lets me leave? What if Jehovah is watching me? What if he wants to commit fornication with me? I was freaking out inside and still trying to pretend I was not scared. "No, I really have to leave, I'll come back later." I pleaded, wishing he'd let go of me. But he pushed his body to mine and kept whispering things in my ear. He pulled me into his bedroom, I tried to resist but not as hard as I should have, I still did not want him to think I was afraid. He began to take my clothes off and I panicked. I tried to push past him to the door but he forcefully held me and threw me on his bed and quickly pulled my pants off of me. After feeling his strength I knew I was trapped. I went limp. He got on top of me. It felt like my skin was ripping. I was trying not to cry but I felt so powerless and humiliated. My legs were tense as I tried to tolerate the invasion. Finally he was done and I shot up the first chance I got. I put my clothes on as fast as I could praying he would not grab me again. He let me leave without a fight. As I left his apartment he said, "Don't get me in trouble, you wanted it too."

As soon as I was out of his view, I ran home. When I got home I got in the shower. My mind would not quit racing. "What if my parents found out I had committed fornication, what if the Elders found out." I was ridden with guilt over what I had done. I knew that it was a sin to not scream if you were being raped, I knew it meant I had wanted it. We were taught as Witness's that if you do not scream during a rape then it is considered fornication. My body burned with fear and shame. Somehow by the time my parents came home I went numb. That night I laid in bed trying to figure out how I could get forgiveness without having to confess to my parents and the Elders. I had been taught that this was the only way to true repentance, which I needed in order to prevent Satan from coming into my life. I was frantic and terrified.

I kept my secret for a couple of weeks. It obsessed my mind and made it almost impossible to get out of bed. But I had to keep going so no one knew anything was wrong. Finally one night my best friend Kim and her mom came over to visit and I confessed to Kim that I had sex. She promised not to tell. I felt a lot better having told someone. Yet I felt bad that I had put Kim in that position. Now she would be *"blood guilty"* for not telling on me. This was another firm rule that Witnesses had to follow. If anyone knew of another's sin and did not tell on them, they were considered just as guilty and would suffer the same wrath as the sinner. Well, the guilt must have got to Kim because a few days later my mom called me downstairs. She told me that Kim's mom had called her and I knew my life was over.

The next thing I knew, I was sitting in a meeting with the Elders. This was the procedure for confessing a sin. The Elders had to determine if you had true repentance so as not to contaminate the whole congregation. The meeting was held in the basement of the Kingdom Hall, our church. It was a small room with bright florescent lighting. Three stern Elders, both of my parents, and I were sitting in a circle on chairs. They began asking me all sorts of questions. They wanted full details of my act of fornication. I was so humiliated and embarrassed. They were angry and disgusted in me. After a long interrogation session they decided to publicly reprove me from the congregation. That meant it would be announced to the entire congregation at the next meeting so everyone would be warned that I was bad association. I also had to be there during the announcement.

After the announcement I could not even hold my head up anymore. I just hated myself for all the horrible things I had done. I began going to school again for fear I would get caught and have more humiliation to deal with. Being away from my bedroom felt like torture to me. That was the only place I felt safe. I began taking antihistamines before I'd leave for school to help me make it through the day. I had been given antihistamines in the past when my ears hurt. They made me feel numb, which was better than I normally felt. I started bringing them to school. I would take one whenever I felt uncomfortable or nervous. It seemed I was taking them at least four times a day. I was walking through life like a zombie. This became too difficult after a few weeks since I could barely hold my head up anymore. I was taking too many pills. I began to feel desperate. I didn't know what I could do to ease the pain anymore. There was no one to turn to.

Around this time I had a very magical experience that has stuck with me through my years. One evening, I was sitting cross legged in the middle of my bed crying thinking such awful thoughts to myself such as, "You are so bad, you don't deserve to be happy because you were born bad, there is nothing you can do about it." These thoughts ran over and over in my mind and suddenly a heat rushed through my body and the thoughts stopped in an instant and were replaced with a calmness unlike I had ever felt. Despite all I had ever been taught by the Witness', somehow I knew I was being embraced by God. My mind was quiet for the first time and a new voice filled my thoughts. It was saying, "You are so loved beyond any love you've ever known, you are good, not a single piece of you is bad, I do not make bad seeds! Feel my love." That is what I did; I sat there until I felt completely filled up with love. It was the most beautiful, peaceful thing I had ever felt.

This experience was against anything that I was taught to believe and I knew if I told anyone, one of two things would happen. Either I would be told I had demons, or they would think I was crazy. I had no explanation to what had happened but I knew it was so real. It was at this moment in my life that I began to question the beliefs of the Jehovah's Witnesses.

My parent's problems were getting worse. They were too wrapped up in their own turmoil to notice mine. When I was fourteen my parents separated. This devastated me. I did not know how to deal with the feelings I was having at the time. My dad left us for another woman and my mom became angry and devastated. She did not want us to see my dad after the awful thing had done to us. She didn't feel he deserved to have his children. I wanted to see him but knew what a betrayal this would be to her. We also left our religion and I knew this meant we would all die in the Tribulation, which scared me to no end.

I had tried to talk to my Dad about how I was feeling just before he had moved out. I told him how sad I felt all the time and how confused I was. I tried to explain to him how I felt, but I found it very hard to explain. I felt like something was wrong with me only I didn't know how to fix it. I wanted to be good so I didn't have to punish myself with mean thoughts and physically hurting myself anymore. My Dad tried to make light of things and told me it was just my age. He did not take me serious. I was losing trust in myself. I started thinking that maybe I was a little crazy. Maybe I just wasn't cut out for life. I did not want to share with anyone else for fear of people thinking I was crazy.

Even my connection to Kim was fading. My older sister had begun hanging out with Kim and I had a lot of jealousy over this. I thought Kim liked her more and this put a wedge between us. Kim had been my only friend and I was grieving over losing her. I remembered first meeting Kim when I was around five or six. Her Uncle Dennis used to baby-sit us while our mothers worked together cleaning houses. But those happy days were long over.

Suicide was often on my mind. I did not know what to do anymore. I kept waiting for things to get better but they never did. I was growing tired. I did not want to feel this way anymore. The emotional pain was the worst. Dealing with my Dad being gone was incredibly traumatic for me. In fact, the entire family was in turmoil over the separation. This was another reason to keep my problems to myself. I did not want to add to the already hard situation.

As my mind became overwhelmed with turmoil, I could feel my spirit leaving me. Finally the day came when I was too devastated to deal with anymore. I took a bottle of allergy pills from the medicine cabinet. I got a big glass of water and started taking the pills as I sat on the toilet crying. I was so confused. I must have taken at least fifty pills. Within minutes, I began feeling sick to my stomach. I went to lay on my Moms bed. After a short time, I started having stabbing pain in my stomach. I immediately felt terrified. The pain was so bad that I thought I was dying. I panicked and realized I wanted to live. What happened after that is still very foggy to me. Somehow my Dad showed up and was sitting next to me on the bed while I threw up profusely. I tried to tell him what I had done, but he told me to just rest. I wanted to go to the hospital. I thought I was going to die.

Finally, I quit throwing up and was able to rest. My Dad and I never discussed it after that.

Shortly after the suicide attempt, I ran away from home. I wanted to escape my pain and did not know how. So one day I walked out the door to go to school and never came back home.

Two

The first day that I decided to run away is still vivid in my mind. I was fourteen years old and in ninth grade. I was on my way to school when I decided I could not face another day. I passed my school and just kept walking. I walked all day thinking of how bad I was and how there was no hope for me. I had tried so hard to be good but I always failed. I was ashamed of who I was. In my mind I somehow convinced myself that if I ran away from my life, the shame would go away. It tortured me so much that I could not bear it any longer. So, with no plan of where I was going or what I was going to do, I walked away from my life that day.

I grew up in the inner city of St. Paul, Minnesota. I went to Central High School, which was located in a rough area of town. I should have been scared as I walked down these streets but I wasn't. Nothing scared me more than going back to my life. I felt nothing. It felt as if I was in a movie, everything around me was surreal. The run down houses, the gangs hanging out on the corners, the cars with tinted windows driving by yelling things to me, none of it scared me. I just walked right through it all. By afternoon I was so exhausted and started to wonder where I was going to sleep. There were several broken down cars in the alleys, if worse came to worse I could hide out in one of them.

A short time later, a tan Cadillac pulled up alongside of me. The window rolled down and a man in the passenger seat started talking to me. I don't remember what he was saying but eventually he asked me if I was on the run. I told him I wasn't, but he knew I was lying. He seemed very concerned about where I was going to sleep. He told me he would help me out just for tonight if I wanted him to. I was relieved and accepted his offer not because I trusted him. I just didn't feel as if I had much to lose at that point. I got in the back seat of the car and we drove away.

The man driving introduced himself as Wolf Dog. He freaked me out a little. He was old and had this sneaky look in his eye with a big crazy looking Afro. He reached back and rubbed my leg. I pushed his hand away and he laughed. The other guy, who was much younger, said his name was Leroy. He seemed much safer. Wolfe, as Leroy called him, drove us to Leroy's apartment. We went in the building and he told me he had to sneak me in since he lived with his dad. He got me in his bedroom without being noticed. He asked me if I was hungry. I was so he went to get me something to eat. After I ate I felt like he was sincere and trusted him. Then I went to sleep.

The next morning Leroy asked me what I was going to do. He wanted to know why I ran away. I wouldn't tell him anything. He tried to convince me to go home but I told him I wouldn't. When he realized I didn't have a plan or anywhere to go, he told me he would help me out but I'd have to be willing to work. I agreed and he called Wolfe to come and pick us up. I had no idea of what he wanted me to do for work but I was so desperate and thankful not to be alone that I didn't care. Leroy said he would take care of me and hide me out if I just did what he told me to. I didn't ask any questions. I didn't even want to know what he had planned. I just followed along.

Wolfe picked us up and we went to a video arcade. He gave me a red towel and told me to go into the little photo booth, drape the red towel as a background, and have my picture taken without smiling. I went in and did as I was told. Then we went to a house where a Mexican guy took my picture and put it in the driver's license of some woman. Somehow they had her purse and all her credit cards. I did not ask any questions even though I was confused and wondered what they were up to. We left there and drove to a big electronic store. They had me memorize the woman's birthday, address, and practice signing her name on the way there. When we got there I was told to go in the store and buy any item over $500.00 with her credit card. Then I got nervous. They both told me not to worry and assured me they did this all the time and never got caught. Leroy reminded me I had no one but him to help me out. I went in the store and purchase an expensive camera. I was shocked that no one questioned me at all.

After that we went to several more stores and I was even able to buy myself some clothes. This went on all day and I was getting really tired but Wolfe insisted we hit one more store. It was a grocery store. I went in and bought a cart full of meat like they told me but this time I was questioned. When they called for the manager and I saw security coming, I ran out as fast as I could. Wolfe pulled right up to the outside of the doors. I jumped in and we sped away. I was shaking so hard. Leroy and Wolfe had an argument. Leroy was mad that he had made me do the last store even though I had told them I wasn't up to it. Leroy told me they would trust me from now on and told me I had done better than anyone he had ever seen.

That night Leroy got in bed with me and we slept together. The next day we did more checks and then Leroy brought me with him to watch him play basketball. This routine went on for about a week. Then one day after basketball Leroy brought me to a friend's house. He told me I was going to stay there for the night because he had stuff to do. His friend was a Mexican man who spoke little English. He told me his friend would take care of me and to do what he told me to. I felt really uncomfortable when Leroy left. The house was dark and dirty. I went into the bathroom to get cleaned up and there was roaches crawling everywhere. I was so mad at Leroy. I asked the guy where I could go to sleep and he pointed towards the stairs. I went up to find it was a little attic area. It was dark besides the moonlight coming through a small window beside a bed. I crawled into the bed and tried to sleep. As I was dozing off I heard someone coming up the steps. I froze pretending to sleep. I saw the outline of the Mexican man coming toward me. He stood beside the bed and unzipped his pants then pulled back my blanket. I could not even believe this was happening. I was trapped and so taken off guard that I did not even fight. I had no idea if this guy would hurt me so I went along. He took off my pants and raped me. When he left, I laid very still for a long time staring out of the little window not sure what to do, but terrified he would come back. Then I quietly got up and crept down the steps and out the back door. That first breath of fresh air felt like total freedom and relief. Even though I had no idea where I was going, I was so glad to be out of that house.

During this period of my life I had saved a couple of the poems I wrote. The following is one of them that I wrote about the night in the little attic room.

Arms of the Night
Gazing at the midnight sky
Hidden tears I cannot cry
Fallen stars streaming down
Lonely beauty all around
Dancing tree tops sway in time
To windy thoughts that haunt my mind
Glimmers of the harvest moon
Cast a soft glow on the gloom
Enough to spy the lonely streets
That crawls with vultures at my feet
I whisper prayers to give me peace
While angel's rock my soul to sleep

I walked down the alley for a few blocks but I did not see any cars I could sleep in. I went back towards the house hoping Leroy would come back. Behind the Mexican's garage was a broken down car. I got in the backseat to wait for Leroy. I fell asleep but was woke up to a loud van pulling up beside the garage. I got out of the car to see if it was Leroy. Three Mexican guys were standing there drinking beer. When they spotted me they all came towards me and began grabbing at my breasts. I asked if they knew Leroy and they talked to each other in Spanish for a minute. Then one of them opened the side van door while the biggest guy grabbed me. I struggled to get away but he threw me into the van. They all got in the back with me and shut the door. The van was carpeted from floor to ceiling in orange carpet, I remember that vividly. The big guy was very rough with me and the other two kept laughing and drinking their beer. I began crying and was obviously terrified but they did not care at all. I thought they were going to kill me and I freaked out. They tore my pants off of me and pinned me down. They took turns raping me. While the big man was on top of me I could not breathe. He had his entire weight on me and I was gasping for air. I knew I was going to die. I went into frenzy but no matter how much I fought with all my strength, I could not budge under his body, so I went limp. I blacked out and when I came to they were throwing me out of the back of the van. Then they drove away.

I did not know where I was. I got up and began walking down the alley. Soon I recognized where I was and I found my way to Leroy's apartment. He was not there so I waited outside the building. Finally as the sun came up, a car pulled up and Leroy got out. As he approached me I started crying and hitting him, I was so angry. He calmed me down and acted shocked at what they did to me. He told me he would get someone after them and they would pay. He snuck me in his room and I slept all day and into the next night. He woke me up and had something for me to eat. Then he told me he was leaving. I just fell back asleep.

The next morning Leroy came in and said we had to get out of there. A ride was waiting for us outside. We drove to the basketball courts and I sat while Leroy played ball. After the game Leroy brought me over to a guy sitting in an old beat up green car. He introduced me to him. He said it was his cousin, Keith. He told me I was going with Keith while he went to get his hair done. I freaked out on him and he promised I would be safe. I did not want to go but I had no options so I got into Keith's car and we drove away. Keith tried to talk to me but I did not talk back. I pretended he wasn't there. He did seem nice enough though so I felt a little calmer. He took me to a beach where a bunch of his relatives were having a picnic. Everyone was really nice and I got to eat good finally. Then Keith tried to bring me back to Leroy but he was nowhere to be found. I started to panic again. Keith asked me if I had anywhere else he could bring me and I started to cry. Then I told him my deal, how I had run away and could not go home. He said I could stay with him and he would try to find Leroy the next day. We never found Leroy and I ended up being with Keith for months. We slept in his car or in a little storage unit under an apartment building.

Soon into my stay with him I was prostituting to support Keith's crack addiction. I thought I was in love with him and that he loved me but I was only 15 and he was 26. Yet I felt a safety with him and I clung to that. Finally I was arrested one day and sent to a group home. The counselors wanted me to talk about things, but I couldn't. It was too painful to feel anything. At least on the streets I didn't have to feel anymore, I just survived. I ran again the first chance I had. I knew by this time how to make money to survive and that is what I did. I also got high every chance I had. Smoking pot was a good way to not feel or think and it helped deal with the awful headaches I lived with daily. I was raped and beat often enough to where it did not scare me anymore, it was just part of being on the street.

Over a three year period I was caught and sent to group homes or hospitals a few times but I always ran when they pushed me to talk. One hospital tried to convince me my dad had sexually abused me, this really freaked me out. I did not know what was real anymore.

When I was sixteen I made an attempt to quit running away. I had been picked up on the streets by the police and after a short stay in juvenile detention, I was sent to live with my mother. I began going to school for my GED. I got a part time job and was trying so hard to deal with life.

I never was able to feel very connected to anyone during my brief stay at home and soon I could not resist the urge to run again. Reality was just too painful. So I ran away again for the last time.

This time I ended up on the streets of New York prostituting for a pimp. He had tricked me into going with him promising to take care of me. When we arrived in New York his lies became apparent when he took everything from my purse that identified me and threw it away. He gave me a new identity and warned me never to use my old name again. He told me I was no longer that person. He also told me I was not allowed to contact my family or anyone from my past again. That very first night he sent me with some other women and they taught me how to work the streets of New York. They watched me every minute and a few times a night our pimp would drive by to collect our money. I was searched to make sure I was not hiding any money from him. This life was terrifying. It was a whole different ball game than the streets in Minnesota. There were frequent murders of prostitutes, a lot of police heat, and weekly trips to the New York City jails. Soon my pimp moved me to Philly where I worked in a massage parlor turning tricks during the day and dancing at a strip club at night. I felt trapped and afraid to escape. He had me watched constantly.

By the age of seventeen, I began feeling really strange. I thought maybe I was going crazy and became very scared. I could not handle being on the run anymore, but I knew getting away from my pimp would be nearly impossible. He had warned me about leaving. Then one night he left me alone in our apartment.

I remember sobbing uncontrollably as I sat on the floor in front of the coffee table staring at my stash of pot in a shoe box top. There was a razor blade in the box. After I thought for hours of how I could make my life better, I decided there was no way out, my life was hopeless. I could not bear my pain anymore and I had nowhere left to hide from it. I picked up the razor and I held it to my wrists and cried so loudly and yelled, "God please help me!" The next thing I remember was waking up on the couch with that calm feeling I had felt on the middle of my bed that one miraculous evening.

I immediately felt a powerful surge of energy and knew again God had taken over my thoughts. They told me I needed to call my mom, I knew clearly and calmly what to do. I called her told her where I was and she told me to hang up and call the police. When they arrived, she told me to have them call her and she would handle it. That it exactly what I did. Within a few days I was on a plane home to my mother. That is how my running ended.

Three

Shortly after I came home, I found Keith. I was looking for some kind of safe feeling or a security. I saw him a few times but it was different. I did not feel in love anymore, just afraid. I never called him again. Soon after all of this I discovered I was pregnant. I decided right then that I was going to change my life and try to be strong. I needed to make things better. I needed to learn to deal with things and not run away from life anymore. I found a determination that I had never experienced before. I was going to have a baby and for the first time I felt as if I had a reason to live.

I spent the next nine months preparing for motherhood. I still had a lot of the same pain I had as a child, but I was so glad to be home after the years I spent on the streets. I just tried to push all the difficulties I was still having out of my mind. My mother and I never discussed much about my running away. I think it was too painful for both of us to talk about. But I did write her several apology letters for the trauma I put her through. I had incredible guilt over that. I also felt awful about leaving my sisters. My older sister had moved out while I was on the run. My younger sister still lived with my mother. I felt as if I had deserted her and did not know how to make up for it. The guilt was very hard to deal with but my family was so supportive and loving to me. I knew I was forgiven I just could not forgive myself.

During the first months of being home and actually feeling safe, I had a lot of nightmares involving men hurting me. I would wake up covered in sweat, thinking I was still on the run. When I looked around and saw I was safe at home I felt relieved. Often during the day I found myself remembering little incidents that happened while I was on the streets and I would get really freaked out. I tried to block it all out of my mind. It is over I would tell myself, let it go.

I found out Kim was also pregnant. I wanted to call her so badly but I was afraid she was mad at me for leaving her when I ran away.

On May 12, 1988, I gave birth to a little girl. Never had I felt such joy as I did when I looked at my baby. I was so amazed at her beauty and perfection. Her birth brought me hope for the first time in my life. Hope of having some happiness and peace, for that is what I felt when I looked at her. When my daughter was one years old, I moved out on my own. I worked as a waitress at night in order to support myself. Living alone with a child at eighteen was hard. I was very lonely. I became involved with a man who I knew from before I had run away. After a short time, I ended up pregnant again. He obviously was not ready to settle down because he disappeared after he found out I was going to have his child. I was not really too worried about having another child alone though. I had been through harder things than that before.

Throughout my pregnancy, I felt tired most of the time. I still had the morning headaches that I had been having since I could remember, but now I had my daughter. I was determined that nothing was going to bring me down. I felt so blessed to be given a child and all of the pride and happiness that goes along with it. I no longer had time for those bad feelings. I had to be a mother now.

On April 6, 1990, I delivered my second child, a healthy baby boy. I fell in love again! I decided that being a mother had to be the most rewarding thing there is in life. I felt as if my children saved my life, they gave me something to live for, a purpose.

Strangely enough, two months earlier Kim also had a baby boy. Her boyfriend was very controlling and I did not get to see much of her since he felt threatened by our friendship.

Shortly after my son was born, my mother and sister moved about an hour away from where I lived. Since I did not have a vehicle, it was hard to go and see them. I felt as if a rug had been pulled out from under me. They had been my only emotional support, besides my older sister who also lived far away from me.

I lived in the inner city in a rough neighborhood. I did not have a phone due to my financial situation. I was a single mother with no phone, which was not a good combination in my neighborhood. I began dealing with a lot of harassment from several men in the area. This was scary since I had no way of getting help if I needed it. There were many times in which rocks were thrown at my second floor bedroom window during the middle of the night. Other times, some of these men would somehow get in my security apartment building and bang on my door. I felt scared and vulnerable most of the time.

Finally, I told my mother what was happening. She brought the kids and I home with her. She lived in a small peaceful town. I loved it and decided that I wanted to raise my kids there. I did not have the money to make a move like this so my mother found me an apartment and paid for my move. I was so grateful to be out of the city.

I worked as a waitress and my younger sister watched my kids while I worked. It was so nice to be near my family again. Everything was perfect, yet I still had this terrible sadness inside of me. Life felt gloomy to me. I could not seem to shake the depression I felt. I pretended to be happy around the kids, which actually was not too hard since they gave me such joy. But deep down I knew things were not right inside of me. I had begun to have these little spells of confusion. It really shook me up because I had no control over it and it seemed to sneak up on me without warning. They never lasted long, just seconds where I would not know what was going on or what I was doing. I started to feel on guard for these spells, often fearing they would get worse or last longer.

About one year after I had moved, I met Brett. He did not mind that I had two children. In fact, he had a daughter of his own who lived with her mother. After a short time dating, we decided to get married. We wanted to wait until we had enough money saved for a nice wedding. Before that could happen though, I became pregnant again. I was a little nervous about this since we had only been together for a short time.

Brett began working all the time. He would be gone until late in the evening and work weekends also. I felt so alone and disconnected from him. We would argue about this. I wanted more time with him and help with the kids, but he felt his job involved making the money and that was that. He always won in the end.

I had completely lost contact with Kim by this point and I missed her so badly. I tried a few times to get in touch with her but her relationship with her kids father was all consuming so I gave up.

When I was about six months pregnant, I went into premature labor. I was put on bed rest and medication to prevent labor from starting again. I had become very sick to the point of being too weak to walk at times. My doctor searched for reasons as to why I was so sick and going into labor so early. He found what we thought was a swollen lymph node in my neck. I had noticed it months before but had never thought to mention it. The doctor became worried that I may have AIDS. This panicked me. Brett and I both underwent testing to rule out AIDS. As we waited for our results, we both thought of the worst. Finally after days of agonizing over it, the results came back normal.

I became frustrated with the small clinic I was going to. I wanted answers and relief from the suffering I was in, so I went to a reputable medical university, the U of M. After a day of being sent from doctor to doctor among the different clinics there, I was told that I had a Branchial Cleft Cyst in my neck that was extremely infected. It was not a swollen lymph node after all. The cyst was the size of a large egg and was filled with infected fluid. I needed it removed to stop my body from going into labor due to the infection. Not to mention it could burst causing worse problems. So at eight months pregnant I went in for surgery to remove the cyst.

When I was taken into the operating room, I was informed that I would be fully awake for the operation. I was not even given a sedative. They did not want to put the baby at risk by medicating me. I was very afraid but I knew I had no choice. I had been sick for months now and was willing to do anything for relief. After the cyst was removed I was sent home to recover, there was no need to recover there since no anesthesia was used. As we drove home I noticed that I felt instant relief from the sick feeling I had been having. It was amazing to me that this infected cyst could cause me all of the misery that it did.

Recovery from the surgery was very fast, and my baby was doing fine. I spent the last month of pregnancy feeling so relieved. I had thought I was going to lose my baby. I was extremely thankful that everything was going to be okay after the months of worry we had experienced.

I gave up trying to get Brett to spend more time with us for a while. I felt guilty and selfish for wanting more from him after he worked so hard all day. But inside I was beginning to feel more and more alone. I wished he would want to be with us more all on his own without me having to ask him but that never happened. It only made him mad when I brought it up.

On February 5, 1993, I went into labor on time. Labor and delivery went smoothly. I had a perfect baby boy. I was happier than I had ever been after that. I had three beautiful children. I thought I had the perfect life after all I had been through.

On September 29, 1993, Brett and I were married. The day of the wedding was a strange day for me. I had spent the night at my mother's house the night before. We planned an evening wedding, so I had all day to get ready. Instead, I slept all day. I was so tired and could not seem to get up. Finally, one hour before I had to be at the church, I woke up and started getting ready. I could not figure out what was wrong with me. I had planned and planned for this day and had been so excited. Why was I so tired now that the big day was finally here?

I got to the church on time and we had a nice wedding. All four of our kids were in the wedding, which made it very amusing.

Brett's daughter was six, my daughter was five, my son was three, and our new baby was just seven months old.

Then the day after our wedding we found out why I was so tired. We were going to have another baby! I was two months pregnant. This came as a huge surprise. I was in shock for a while and did not really know how to feel about this. Brett and I had just bought a very old house, a fixer upper. We had planned to remodel as we had the money for it.

After a couple of months went by, I started getting excited about the baby. I had decided that if God did not think I could handle another child, then it would not have happened. This pregnancy went well. I was exhausted a lot and still struggled with some depression and my headaches but I knew I had a family to raise and I tried to ignore my troubles.

One of the good things about having three young children, is you do not have a lot of time to dwell on things. They keep you too busy to be worried about anything for very long. I needed this distraction to keep me from worrying about the confusion spells I was having. They were getting more frequent. I never mentioned them to my doctor. Mostly because they were very hard to describe. Secondly, I was a little afraid that I was going crazy. I felt like if I did not talk about it or think about it, then it would go away. At the time, this seemed to me like the only way I could deal with it.

Throughout all of this time, I was still suffering from chronic ear infections. I ignored them also, until the pain would get unbearable, then I would go to the doctor. I would be put on an antibiotic, but as soon as I was done with the prescription, the infections would come back. I was very frustrated with this. I felt like my pain would never end. It was not just the pain. It was the sick, fatigued feeling you get along with an infection that really was getting to me. I had too much responsibility in my life to be dealing with these constant infections. My doctor sent me to a specialist, an ENT doctor. This doctor did nothing different for me. He did not have any answers. So I quit going to him. My prenatal doctor encouraged me to find a different ENT doctor. He was very concerned but I did not follow his advice at the time.

Brett and I still did not have much time together. I was becoming very bitter that I did everything for the kids. His business was picking up and he was making more money but it did not slow him down. It was even more reason for him to work a lot. I also felt resentful that Brett did not trust me with our money. He gave me such a limited amount to live on and it seemed very unfair to me. Brett was always concerned that I would buy things we really didn't need. He would get mad every time I came home from grocery shopping at how much I spent. Even when I had to ask for money to get diapers he would get crabby at me. I began hating to spend money. I hated answering to him, and I could barely stand how he treated me when he was mad. He didn't yell, he would slam stuff and stomp around and snap at the kids. I always felt like his bad moods were my fault.

Before Brett would get home from work every day, I got very nervous and frantically picked up the house. I just hated when he was crabby. When he got home I tried to keep the kids quiet and out of his way so he wouldn't be set off. Usually this didn't work well and he found something to be mad at me about.

On July 6, 1994, I delivered a sweet little girl. Again I felt blessed! Brett and I had decided during my pregnancy, that I would have a tubal ligation done the day after I delivered the baby. I felt very unsure of this decision. I didn't know if I wanted to be done having kids yet. Logically, I knew I should not have any more. Our plate was full already, compared to our financial situation. But deep inside of me I felt wrong for having the surgery. Despite my mixed feelings, I went ahead and had my tubes tied any ways.

Upon awaking from my surgery, I was in excruciating pain in my stomach. I felt as if I could not move because it was so extreme. The nurse gave me a shot, but it did nothing. I knew something was wrong. I could feel it in my heart that something had gone wrong. I expressed this to the nurse but was ignored. I wanted my doctor to come and check on me, but he only told the nurse to give me another shot for pain. Finally after several shots, it subsided. I still had a lingering bad feeling about my surgery the next day but was too embarrassed to question my doctor about it. I did not want him to think I was paranoid. So I just took my pain medication and kept my mouth shut.

Things were pretty hectic around the house with four little ones. During Christmas of 1994, three of them had the chicken pox so we stayed home. The baby was only five months old and she was so sick. I remember breast feeding her and feeling so terrible as I looked at her little face covered in chicken pox. I also felt really sick, and thought that I had a touch of the flu or something.

Days went by and the kids all got better, but I was feeling worse. It was an oddly familiar sick feeling. I felt pregnant. I knew I was being paranoid. I couldn't be pregnant. I had my tubes tied just five months earlier. But I went and bought a home pregnancy test any ways. After having four babies so close together, I was pretty familiar with how it felt to be pregnant and I needed to be sure.

I took the test at my older sister's house. I had a feeling I did not want to be alone for this. Surprisingly, my sister did not think I was crazy for wanting to do this, at least she did not act like it. I took the test and it was positive! I was confused. I kept trying to figure out what was going on. If my tubes were tied, how was I pregnant?

I called my doctor. He told me that it had to be a false positive result. He said there was no way I could be pregnant since the only way it could happen after a tubal ligation, is if the tubes were to grow back together over a period of years. It had not been long enough for this to be happening to me. I decided to buy another pregnancy test. I went home and waited for Brett to get home from work. When he arrived I told him what was going on. He was speechless. I went into the bathroom to take the second test. By this time, I had put a lot of thought into this and had decided that if I truly was pregnant, it had to be some kind of mishap like an egg stuck in my tubes or something. I began to think of the bad feeling I had before my tubal. I wondered if I had made a mistake by having my tubes tied. My biggest fear was that I had altered fate. Maybe I was meant to have one more child.

The second test was again positive. My heart sank, not because I was pregnant but because I thought I would surely miscarry since my tubes were blocked. I fell to the bathroom floor and cried. I cried for the sadness of this child who could have been born but because of me would now die. I was devastated and filled with guilt. Brett calmed me down and convinced me that maybe by some miracle that the egg made it into my uterus and would live. I held on to this hope and prayed for this to be true.

My prayer was answered the next day when I went into my doctor to have this mysterious pregnancy investigated. Brett and I sat in the little room awaiting the doctor for a long time. We heard a lot of whispering outside of the door. Finally the doctor came in. He looked very nervous, which worried me. He sat down and was silent for a minute and then proceeded to tell me that something had gone wrong during my tubal ligation surgery. Apparently they missed one of the tubes. Instead, they cut an artery, which they had mistaken for my fallopian tube. They knew this because the pathology report indicated that the tube clipping that was sent for testing after my surgery, was found to be that of an artery, not a fallopian tube. The reason the doctor did not know this information until now, was because he never read the pathology report, it was just put in my chart. He had just read it before he had entered the room to see me.

So, I was indeed pregnant again. I was a little concerned about what kind of artery was cut and if it would cause a problem for me, but the doctor assured me that it would not hurt me at all.

The thought of having five children, six counting my stepdaughter, was terrifying to me. What a huge responsibility it seemed to be! I began to contemplate motherhood very seriously now. I decided that I needed to be the perfect mother no matter what the cost. Especially since I felt like I was in it alone. Brett made the money but as far as being there for me, he did not have it in him. I was tired of fighting for more from him. Why couldn't he just want to be there for me? I felt like he hated me sometimes, the way that he was always angry. I also felt like he had no trust in me. He controlled everything. I did not even trust myself anymore.

Four

I grew up thinking that adults were perfect, that they were never wrong. I think this misconception really impacted me in a negative way. I'm still waiting for this perfection to come over me. I guess that is why I sometimes feel as if I'm a child trapped in an adult body. I think if I would have known that no one is perfect and that it was okay and normal, I would have probably been more accepting of my mistakes and myself.

Now that I was going to have five, I wanted to find a way to be in tune with my own kids. I wanted to be approachable and the only way to achieve that was to let my kids know that I'm really just like them, only bigger.

Throughout my fifth pregnancy, I had a lot of mixed feelings. I was feeling very nervous about having another baby and guilty for having doubts. It wasn't that I would not love this child, I just didn't know how much more I had to give. I was already at my limit with responsibility. My kids were all so young and needed me constantly. I was becoming very angry that my doctor had made such a mistake at my expense. I had so much on my mind because of this, that I could not fully enjoy the precious young months of my new baby the way I wanted to. My anger was not just at my doctor. I was also angry that my ears hurt all the time and that I was always tired. I was angry that life was so damn hard!

Brett seemed farther away mentally than ever. He was angry that I never wanted sex. He would stay mad at me for days over this. I was too sick and tired and stressed to even think of anything but sleep at bedtime. Brett never seemed to just try to be affectionate with me and I needed that so badly. I did not approach him either, I was too afraid. He always seemed angry. I tried to tune him out so I could function. His moods affected me in such a negative way that blocking him out was the only way I could be okay for the kids.

I became very anxious towards the end of my pregnancy. I was having a lot of trouble with my ears and had recently started having abdominal pain after meals. My doctor thought I was having gallbladder attacks. That was the last thing I needed. I could not handle any more stress at that point. I was barely coping as it was.

My mind was on overload. I was thinking strange things such as, the thought that God was punishing me for being such a bad person. I really believed this. I could not reason out why things were so hard for me and figured this had to be why my life was so filled with pain and struggle. I was also feeling very paranoid. One day I actually had myself convinced that my doctor and my dentist were conspiring with each other to kill me. It sounds crazy now, but in my mind, it felt so real. I had to go to the dentist to have a tooth pulled because it was abscessed. I was so afraid he was going to kill me by using too much gas or something.

It did not help that I had not had a full night sleep in years. My kids were born so close together, by the time I had one sleeping through the night, another was born and waking me for feedings. I was sleep deprived, but there was nothing I could do about it. There was no napping in my crazy house.

After all of the suffering I had endured due to this unexpected pregnancy, I decided to hire an attorney to try to get some sort of compensation for the mistake that was made during my tubal ligation. I was getting angrier, the more time went on. I felt as if my whole life was falling apart. I blamed the doctor who did my tubal wrong. I knew it was awful to be mad at him, but I could not help it. I had some guilt over taking legal action. But I kept thinking of how much harder my life was going to get with another child.

I felt like I needed some sort of help. I tried to research other legal cases that were similar to mine. It was then that I realized just how rare it was for this type of mistake to be made. I could only find a few documented cases of wrongful birth and none of them were due to a tube being missed. I wondered if I was the only one this had ever happened to. I began to think that if something this farfetched could happen to me, than anything could happen.

I became very on guard, just waiting for bad things to happen. It wasn't that I felt having a baby was a bad thing. It was being pregnant, dealing with the ear infections, the stomach pain, the depression, the confusion spells, the paranoid thoughts, the headaches, the constant fatigue, and an angry husband who was never home. All this on top of trying to be a good mother to four little ones. The work involved in that alone was enough to make a person lose it! I did not know how I could possibly handle another child.

The last month of my pregnancy, my cervix was dilated to five. Usually once you are dilated past three, you are in full-blown labor. I was miserable. My daughter was only one year old and still needed to be carried a lot of the time. My body was sore from all of the extra strain. Finally, a few days after my due date, my doctor decided to induce labor. I was in tears constantly by then and could not handle much more.

It was September 7, 1995. I was very ready to be done with pregnancy! I felt as if I had been pregnant my whole life. After a few hours of labor, I delivered a baby boy. I did not know how I would feel to finally see him. I held him right away and breast-fed him. As I looked at his little face, I knew instantly that he was no mistake! He had this strangely familiar look about him, a very comforting look. In my heart I knew that he was sent to me for a reason, I did not yet know why, but I knew he was somehow a part of the plan. The feelings I had towards this baby were very strong, and I immediately knew that I needed him as much as he now needed me.

I was so relieved to be done with this long, hard pregnancy. Even though I had such a deep love for this baby, I still pursued legal matters with the hospital. Now I was doing it for him and the other children. It felt like the right thing to do. We never went to court. When the baby was four months old, we settled with the hospital for a fair amount of money. It was not an astounding amount, but enough to make me feel as if I had been compensated fairly for all I had been through. Although at that point, my baby was reward enough, the money was a bonus.

I put the money away in savings. I was waiting to figure out what I was supposed to do with it. I knew I had to use it for some kind of good and I knew I was not letting Brett decide for me. He had controlled all the money he made, it was my turn to do something. After much thought, I came up with an idea. I decided to start a business that would allow me to be with my children and still earn some money. Then I would not have to ask Brett for money or feel guilty for everything I bought. I was going to open a preschool/day care center.

I spent the next year preparing to open my business. I took a home correspondence course to get my early childhood degree. I planned to incorporate a preschool program into my day care. I converted our double car garage into a child's dreamland. I had a kitchen and bathroom added on, and a lot of open play space. I purchased toys and equipment galore. I did not spare anything. This was my dream and it had to be perfect. I used most of the money I had from my settlement. Brett was not too happy about that, but I felt as if that was what the money was for. This project took a while to complete. Since the garage was not connected to the house, we had to have plumbing and electrical put into the building.

I felt pretty good during the process of getting the day care ready. It took about a year. I was enjoying my children so much. I found that having five was not so bad after all. I actually loved it! I was feeling a lot of pride, not only in the children, but also in myself. I felt like I had a goal that I was working towards, like I had found some sort of purpose in life. I was determined that I was going to provide a wonderful, loving day care where I would be making a difference. I was so excited to share something that I knew I was good at, being a mother.

Brett seemed to be getting more and more down the closer I got to my goal. Finally one day he told me he was afraid if I was financially independent, I wouldn't need him anymore. I assured him it would only help us and that I wasn't going to leave him.

In September of 1997, Kiddie Cottage was open for business. I was very eager to start my preschool program. Soon, my day care was full and I bonded very quickly to all the kids I was caring for. It felt so great to spend my days surrounded by children who looked up to me and loved me. I did my best to give them my all.

In October, I had another ear infection. I knew I could not let the infection get any worse or I'd have to take time off and I had only opened the day care one month earlier. I went in to the doctor and got on medication to clear up the infection. I was fed up with having these infections so I made an appointment at The University of Minnesota to see an ear specialist the following week.

After a few days, I started having clear fluid leaking out of my ear. I was feeling worse. I became very ill with vomiting and diarrhea and I was so lethargic. It happened so fast that I had no time to find someone to help in the day care. I kept working, but it felt like torture to even stand. I was very weak. After a week of this and no sign of getting better, I went to my doctor again. My sister brought me in since I was too weak to drive. I told him I'd had diarrhea for over a week and felt dehydrated. He did not do anything for me. He thought I was depressed. In fact he took my sister in the hall and asked her if I was losing it. She got very upset by this and took me home right away. He was not taking me seriously at all. This was the same day I was scheduled to go in for my appointment at the U of M ear clinic. I was not going to go since I was so ill, but for some reason I suddenly decided I better keep the appointment.

Brett drove me to my ear appointment. By this time I was feeling even worse. My head was hurting so badly and my legs were feeling heavy. A few times, on the drive there, I thought I was going to faint. When a doctor saw me, I was tearful. I felt too weak to talk. This doctor was very nice to me, unlike the one I saw earlier. He tried to comfort me and asked what was wrong. I told him about my experience at the doctor's office earlier that day and how sick I had been. This doctor was an intern in his last weeks of internship. He went to discuss my situation with the head doctor.

Then I was put into a different room that had a special kind of microscopic that could look very deep into the ears. The doctors looked in my left ear and immediately saw my problem. I had a tumor that was growing through my eardrum and out of my ear canal. The doctor explained to me that I had what is called a Cholesteatoma, or tumor. This is a very rare condition that is thought to be caused by chronic ear infections. I also had a very bad mastoid infection. The mastoid is the bone behind the ear and area around it. I was scheduled to have surgery to remove the tumor. The doctor put me on an antibiotic first to try and clear up the infection before surgery. He also gave me medication for the diarrhea that he thought was caused from all of the antibiotics I had been on recently. My surgery would be done two weeks from then.

This news was so unexpected. I had never heard of Cholesteatoma before then and was very afraid of what was happening. I wondered how bad it was. The doctor said we'd find out during surgery. I was not only sick now, but I was an emotional wreck also. What else could possibly happen to me?! Why do all these weird, rare things happen to me? Especially when I just opened my day care. How was I going to have a surgery and still keep my business going? All these questions played over and over in my mind.

The two weeks before my surgery were extremely difficult for me. I needed to still run my day care, in which I had over eight children to care for, plus take care of my own family. I was very tired and sick. By the time I went in for surgery, my infection had still not cleared up and I had been having the clear fluid draining from my ear again. It seemed that whenever I had this drainage, I also felt very lethargic and strange. I didn't know what this fluid could be, but I knew it wasn't good.

On November 24th, 1997, I went in to have my tumor removed. I was very nervous, yet eager to feel good again. I was very hopeful that this tumor was causing all my problems. I believed that my confusion spells were related to the tumor. I was so excited that I was going to be normal, that I was going to feel good soon. I had my older sister watching over my day care. The doctor said that I would only have some mild discomfort after surgery and could go home that same day. I had planned to take a couple of days to recover. I was happy that my business would not be too disrupted by all of this.

I was prepped for surgery and then taken to the operating room. That is all I remember until I woke up. As I awoke, I noticed a terrible pain all over my head. I had never felt anything like it before. I felt like my head was going to burst, it felt so tight. I remember crying for pain medication. The nurse seemed confused, but she could tell I was really in a lot of pain and asked the doctor if she could give me a shot. I thought I was going to die. The pain shot did not help. Soon I was given another, and another, until I was forced to fall asleep even amidst the pain I was still in. As I dozed off, I quit breathing. The recovery nurse woke me and decided to sit right next to me and make sure I kept breathing. She had to shake me several times to awake me. My body was not breathing on its own like it was supposed to. I had to consciously think about making myself breathe. This was so difficult because I could hardly keep my eyes open with all of the pain medication I had been given. I just wanted to sleep. I wanted to forget the pain I was in. I wanted Brett. The nurses would not let him in to see me yet.

My doctor came in to see me. He informed me that my tumor had been much larger than they anticipated, because of this they had to do a different, more extensive procedure. It had taken them almost four hours to remove everything that was damaged. The tumor was wrapped around my facial nerve and all the small bones in my ear. The bones were destroyed by the tumor and had to be removed also. Basically, everything in my ear and mastoid area was removed. The doctor told me that everything was inflamed and bleeding and very infected. I was also informed that the tumor would most likely recur.

Finally, several hours later, they let Brett come in. I began to cry with relief. I had been in so much pain with no one to comfort me for so long. Just seeing Brett brought comfort to me. Brett was shocked at how swollen my face was. I was almost unrecognizable. My head was bandaged and I was crying from the pain. The nurse explained to him that my breathing needed to be watched. All of this was not what we had been prepared for, and Brett seemed worried. I believe he knew as much as I did that something was not right.

Shortly after this, I was moved to a different room to recover. Late that evening, a nurse came in and informed us that they were closing the day surgery area of the hospital and that we would need to leave now. I told her I was still in extreme pain and did not feel as if I could make it home. The nurse went to get the head nurse.

When she came in my room, she appeared very annoyed. I expressed to her also that I could not leave. I told her that I was in too much pain still. At hearing this, the women told me in a very firm voice that the type of surgery I had underwent did not cause such pain, only mild discomfort. She seemed to be challenging my honesty. This upset me. I told her that after having gone through labor five times with no pain medication, I thought I knew the difference between pain and discomfort, and I was definitely in pain. She then became even more irritated with me. She explained to me that if they were to put me in a hospital room, it would be very expensive since we did not have any medical insurance. She also suggested renting a nearby hotel room. It was clear to me then what this was all about, money! I was not only in extreme pain, now I was also humiliated and mad. I began to cry. I was so tired and frustrated with the pain. I knew something was not right. I wanted my doctor to come and see me, but he was gone. I was being treated so rudely, that I did not want to be there no matter how awful I was feeling. Brett brought me home.

Once I was home, I could rest much better. I stayed at my mother's house for a couple of days to recover before going home to all the kids. Two days after my surgery, I still was feeling very weak and I could tell I was going downhill. As I was lying on my mother's bed, I felt something wet under my ear. When I sat up to check, the pillow was covered in blood. I could feel the blood running down my neck. I put my hand over my ear and went to get my mother. My two sisters were sitting in the kitchen with my mom. When they saw me they jumped up and ran over to me. The shoulder of my white t- shirt was covered in blood. My mom bandaged my ear and I called the hospital. I explained to the on call ENT doctor that my ear was bleeding. He told me that this could be normal after the type of surgery I had. I explained to him that it was bleeding quite a lot, but he still did not seem to be concerned.

After a few of days went by, I still did not feel well enough to take care of my day care, but I felt as if I had no choice. I did not want to call the parents this soon after opening. So I tried to act as if I was fine. I went through the next few days in a fog. I had a lot of drainage coming from my ear. It was greenish and had a terrible smell. I could not believe I had so much junk in my ear. I was soaking a cotton ball every few minutes. I was also becoming weaker, I felt as if I barely had the strength to move. I remember lying on the floor of the day care and feeling as if I was going to die.

On December 2, 1997, one week after my surgery, I woke feeling very weird. Something strange was happening to me, I knew that much, I just did not know exactly what was happening. I went into my day care to prepare for the kids to come. At this point, it felt like torture to even be out of bed. I was completely fatigued and still in so much pain. My entire head hurt like it was being squeezed so tightly. As I stumbled through the door, I began to vomit. I had to crawl to the bathroom because the strength in my legs was gone. I kept vomiting, with each heave, my head felt as if it would explode. The pain was unbearable. One of my day care children then showed up. I somehow made it out of the bathroom to greet him. The mother kept asking me if I was okay. I told her I'd be fine, and that I was going to call my older sister to come and help me. She left and I curled up on some pillows and watched the little one play. As I watched him, I prayed for the strength to take care of him. But, I was soon back in the bathroom vomiting. After I was done, I again had to crawl to get to the phone. I knew I needed help. I called my sister and asked her if she could come over. She said she had an errand to run and would come over after. I waited for her to get there, but after a couple of hours, I became very afraid. I felt like I was dying. Everything was covered in a white haze. I remember thinking that I was very close to the other side, the spirit world. I felt as if there were so many spirits in the room with me. I could feel the comfort they were sending me, but it was clear to me that they could not help me. I kept having these visions of heaven in my mind. It felt as if I was being warned that I was headed in that direction if I did not get help. This message I was receiving was strong, somehow I knew it was from whoever was with me, my angels, spirits, or maybe God. I didn't know who it was but the feelings were powerful. I had never experienced anything like this before. I felt like my physical body was fading away and as I became weaker I was growing closer and more in tune to this spiritual realm I was experiencing. This scared me because whoever was sending these thoughts to me must have known me well enough to know how I usually ignore my physical symptoms. They knew I would not seek help if I were not shown the serious danger I was in.

I could not be alone any longer. I called my other sister. I don't know what I said but she sensed the urgency. Soon, both of my sisters were there. My older sister called my ENT doctor to see what we should do. His nurse got on the line and asked to talk with me. I got on the phone and asked my sister to leave the room. I told the nurse that I was dying, I told her I was starting to hear Angels. She told me to come in by ambulance right away.

It was a forty-minute drive from my house to the hospital and I needed to be with my family in case I did not make it. I did not want to take an ambulance. My sister called Brett so he could drive me in. As we drove to the hospital, I laid in the back seat vomiting.

When we arrived, I was too weak to walk. I was taken to see my doctor by wheel chair. When the doctor looked in my ear and saw all of the blood and drainage and noticed how dehydrated I was, he seemed a bit panicked. He rushed to get an IV started of fluids and two different antibiotics. The infection had spread into both ears and possibly into my brain. I was admitted into the hospital and given several blood tests. A culture of my ear was tested to find out what strain of germ I was infected with.

By that night, I was feeling incredibly better. The nurse that I had talked to on the phone came to see me. After telling her about the week I'd had, she was outraged that I was sent home after my surgery. She said that I was treated so poorly and it could have cost me my life. I knew this already, but it was nice to have this validation. She was pretty shook up from our phone conversation. She needed to come and see me and make sure I was okay. I was very touched by that.

After spending a few days in the hospital, I felt very rested and almost well enough to go home. Then my test results came back with some bad news. It turned out that the germ infecting my ears was a bacteria that is very hard to kill. It only responded to one particular antibiotic, which is the strongest, most expensive antibiotic there is. Not only that, but I also had three other strains of different bacteria infecting my ears. It was like having four ear infections at once. Even worse though, was the fact that the only effective way to kill the infection was to have the medicine go through an IV into my heart. My infection had gotten so out of control that I was going to have to administer this medicine myself at home since I would need to be on it for weeks. An IV, called a PICC line, was inserted through a vein in my arm leading to my heart. The drug was more effective going directly to my heart. I was shocked at how serious this had become. I never knew an ear infection could lead to such trauma. I was given training on administering IV antibiotics. It was scary because if I were to make one mistake, it could be very serious. I had no choice though. Another shock was the fact that we had to purchase the medicine for my PICC line, which was $104.00 per day, and we did not have medical insurance at the time.

Finally, after five days, I was sent home. I missed my kids so much. They were very happy I was back. Five days without me had put my house in total chaos! It was nice to really see how much I was needed, yet a little hard to come home to such disorganization. My kids were all very needy. They had been worried they were going to lose me.

I spent the next five weeks administering the IV antibiotics. Every week I went in to my ENT doctor hoping he would be able to remove the PICC line, only to be told I'd have to come back the next week because the infection was still too severe to remove the IV. It was really starting to bother me after five weeks of this. My skin was very sore around the needle. My doctor was worried it was getting infected. An infection there would be very bad since it was a vein leading directly to my heart. So my IV was finally removed on the fifth week. My infection was much better by this point and I was given an oral medication.

The shock of this near death experience had left me in a state of disbelief. I almost felt as if I should be taking things harder than I actually was. In order to keep functioning with my life, my kids, my day care, and my health, I needed to detach from the situation emotionally. I did not consciously choose to do this, it just happened. It is an incredible thing how our body's natural defense mechanism knows exactly when to kick in when life gets too hard. I was feeling very little concern. Actually, I was not feeling much of anything! Besides, I figured things could not get any worse than what they were- or so I thought!

Five

My shock did not last too long. Soon, I was back to running my day care and reality hit me! Everything felt very different now. I had dreamed of opening this business for so long and had ideas of how it was going to be, but never did I expect I'd go through all of these health problems. It changed things for me. Instead of my focus being on the kids and my dream of having the best preschool program around, I found myself having difficulties with everyday tasks.

My intuition was telling me that something inside of me was not right. I could not put my finger on what it was exactly, but I knew I felt very different than I had before my ear surgery. It was very hard for me to make any decisions, and I would become frustrated with myself. Things that came naturally to me before, were hard to figure out now. I had to think very hard about everything I did like getting my kids ready for school or grocery shopping. I use to have a system, a routine, but now I could not remember how I did it. Every little thing I had to do felt very overwhelming. It was even worse when unexpected things were thrown into my day, like if one of my kids got sick and needed to go to the doctor. With five kids there were many unexpected things. I found myself crying a lot because my mind felt so overloaded with decisions that I could not seem to think out and process. I wondered what was happening to me. I use to have it together, at least as much as a mother of five can. I felt like I was drowning in life.

Within a couple of months from my surgery, I began to have a problem keeping my balance. I first noticed it when I would wake up during the night to tend to the kids. I would bump into the walls and trip a lot. I could not walk straight no matter how hard I tried. Soon it became apparent during the daytime also. I was having a hard time just walking across a room. Along with this, I would get dizzy.

I went in to see my ENT doctor about this. He told me that my surgery should not cause any of the symptoms I was having. He checked my ears and did some tests but could not find any reason as to why I was having balance problems. He told me to call him if it did not get better soon. I was very discouraged not to have any answers. I knew something was wrong and felt very nervous that even my doctor was baffled by my symptoms.

When it did not get any better I decided to see my family doctor. I told him how I was feeling. After talking with my ENT doctor, he ordered a MRI to see if I may be having problems where my tumor had been. The MRI came back normal. My doctor told me I was having anxiety.

I was trying to be optimistic. I kept telling myself that nothing was going to get in the way of my dreams. My day care business was doing so well despite my health issues. I was able to keep it a secret from everyone and was praying for my mental and physical problems to just go away on their own before they became obvious. I told myself I was just healing and it would all be fine, but deep down I knew this was not true.

My days were long and exhausting. I started my day getting my oldest two children up and ready for school. Then I would wake my little three who were not the most cooperative, and try to get them dressed and ready to go out into the daycare building. By 7:30, my first day care kids were arriving. Then I fed everyone breakfast and began my preschool routine. At 6pm, my daycare children were gone and I had to quickly make dinner for my family. My evenings consisted of housework, laundry, homework, bath time, quality time with each of my kids, grocery shopping, daycare paperwork, and so much more. During all of this, I felt like a maniac. Keeping everything straight was impossible. My headaches were really bad, now they were lasting throughout my whole day. I do not even remember Brett being around much and when he was the tension in the house was unbearable.

I began having heart palpitations. Several times a day, my heart would just start beating very hard and fast. Other times I would notice a few hard thumps in my chest. When I would lie down to go to sleep, my chest felt extremely heavy and the fast heart beating would start. As I would doze off, I'd quit breathing and wake up gasping for air. This started happening several times a night. These symptoms were scary. I had never had anything like this happen to me. I went to my regular family doctor again to have it checked out. I told him all of the strange symptoms I had been having. He seemed to still think I was just stressed out. I would have loved to believe that but I knew it was more than that. He was not willing to do anything else for me, he was sure nothing was wrong. I was angry with this. I felt as if I was just pushed aside and not taken seriously, but there was nothing else I could do about it. It is hard to argue with a doctor especially when you do not really know what is going on either. You just have to trust them.

I was feeling pretty sick also. I felt as if I had the flu all of the time. I was weak and fatigued. Brett was tired of all of my complaints. He had been listening to them since shortly after our wedding. It seemed as if my health had been going downhill since then. I tried very hard not to say anything about how I was feeling to Brett. When I did he would get very mad at me. He thought I was just being negative. I do not think he believed there was anything wrong with me at first. I felt as if I had to deal with all of these scary feelings I was having alone. I went to bed every night terrified I would die in my sleep. Every night I prayed for relief, but it never came.

During fishing opener that year in May, I decided to meet Brett up north with my sister, Gabbi. On the way up north I told Gabbi all of the crazy things going on with me. She told me she had felt similar before her brain surgery a couple years before. I wondered if we had the same brain condition. I was so confused.

Shortly after this, in May of 1998, six months after my ear surgery, I began having fainting spells. It started as a lightheaded feeling would wash over my body, I felt as if I was drifting away from consciousness. Within seconds everything turned black and I would lose all feeling in my body. The spells lasted only a minute or so but left me with a lingering weakness and inability to concentrate on anything. These spells also left me with a terrible fear to go anywhere. I could not find any reason for the spells, they did not seem to be related to any activity I was doing. I did not know how I could prevent them or have any warning to when they were going to happen. I tried not to have to leave my house for fear of this.

On May 17th, I had to make a trip to the grocery store. As I walked in the door, the feeling began to come over me. I grabbed a man who was walking past me. I could hardly speak, I was feeling so weak and faint. I tried to tell him I was going to faint. He yelled for help. I think I lost consciousness for a few seconds. When I opened my eyes, I was leaning over a cart and a lady who worked at the store was holding on to me tightly. She was asking me if I needed an ambulance. I said no, I was thinking of the fact that we had no insurance and how expensive an ambulance would be. The woman took me to sit in back and gave me some orange juice. Meanwhile someone called my sister to come and get me. The next day, I went back to my ENT doctor. I did not know where else to turn. Upon hearing all of my new symptoms, my doctor told me he was going to send me to his own personal doctor who was very knowledgeable. She was an internal medicine doctor at the U of M. He arranged for me to see her that day despite her month long waiting list. I was very grateful and also hopeful that I would finally get some answers and possibly relief.

As I waited to see the doctor, I began to feel faint once again. I asked the nurse to check my blood pressure. It was 90/50, which was very low for me. It was then that I realized that my feelings of faintness were related to my blood pressure dropping. When the doctor came in, I told her all of the symptoms I had been having since my ear surgery. I explained to her that strange new symptoms seemed to keep arising, such as the fainting. She asked me what my family medical history was. I explained that my younger sister had Arnold Chiari Malformation, a brain disorder.

I did not know anything about the condition. My sister had a MRI done the year before due to a work injury. The MRI showed this malformation and all we were told by her doctors, was that she needed brain surgery to treat her condition. I asked my doctor if she thought I could possibly have this condition. She did not think my symptoms were that of a brain disorder. I then told her my other sister had Grave's disease, a thyroid disorder. She did not think that could be my problem either. She asked to come back the next day for a full physical since she did not have time then.

During my physical the following day, the doctor discovered that my heartbeat sounded irregular. She informed me that she was almost positive that I had pulmonary hypertension. If that were so, I would need to be treated immediately as it could be fatal. She told Brett and I that all of my symptoms fit with this diagnosis. I was sent to the hospital for an echocardiogram, which would look at my heart. I was so excited to have an answer. Even though it sounded serious, at least now I could be treated and get some relief from all of the suffering I was going through.

After the test, I was sent home. I was very confused as to why I was not kept in the hospital since my doctor was so sure that we had found my problem. I asked what my test results were, but no one could tell me anything. I was told that my doctor would be calling me within a few days. I left feeling extremely down hearted. I was expecting to get some relief. I was going home with no hope in sight, again!

I was so tired of dealing with all of this. It was awful trying to keep up my day care and trying to take good care of my own kids when I felt so sick. I knew something terrible was wrong inside of my body and just when I had hope of figuring things out, I was sent home to dwell on all of the awful possibilities. What if I die because they sent me home?

What if the doctor was wrong and I'm back at square one? What if I feel like this forever? What if I am going crazy? I couldn't take it anymore. It had been six months of this and it was getting worse each day. I thought when you got sick, you went to the doctor, they told you what was wrong, and then give you medicine or something to fix it. I was finding out how wrong I was about this. The doctor's did not know everything and that was a scary thought!

After a few days went by, I still had not heard back from the doctor. It was like torture to keep waiting, so I called to find out how my test had turned out. I could not talk to my doctor but her nurse got on the phone and told me that my test results were fine. She said that my doctor would call me as soon as she had a chance. I was very angry. How could they let me sit not knowing what was going on? If my test was fine, then what was wrong with me!?

My life was feeling so pointless. I could barely function any more. I had no hope to hold on to. No hope of this nightmare I was living through ending. How could I live with no hope? Every night I prayed the same prayer. I begged God to heal me. I begged for hope. I prayed that my children would forgive me for not being the mother they deserved. Every morning when I awoke, my heart sank as I realized that I was not healed. I still could hardly drag myself out of bed. I would cry as I got up every day, often times asking God why he would not just help me. My faith was being shaken by this terrible sickness that was overtaking my life. Here is an excerpt from my journal during this time:

Journal: May 26, 1998
I'm getting so tired of having these spells. They are terrifying! I feel like I've lost all independence. I can't even drive and feel safe. I 'm afraid I will pass out behind the wheel. I wish I knew what was wrong with me. I can't live like this! This is not how I'm supposed to be. I had plans for my life. I wanted to be a writer, a poet, a normal person. Is that asking too much, to just follow my dreams? To be the person I was meant to be?

I need to have hope or life is not worth living. God, help me to find some hope, help me to find some answers. I cry at bedtime, I cry when I awake. I feel my spirit growing weak. I'm sick all the time and so tired. What is happening to me?! I'm fighting to keep my will to live. The doctors have no answers, they think I'm crazy. I'm starting to wonder if that is true! I've even seen spiritual healers, they too, are unable to help me. No one has the answers, no one knows what is wrong! God, you are my only hope now. Please give me a miracle. Are you even with me, Lord? Please show me a sign...

About one month after my appointment with the doctor who had sent me for the tests, she finally called me. The phone call was incredibly disturbing. She told me she thought I was having severe anxiety, maybe due to my job and having so many children of my own. She asked me to try taking an antidepressant drug for one month and if it did not help she would see me again. I reluctantly agreed. I could see that she did not believe me. I tried to tell her that I felt it was more than anxiety causing my problems. I asked her if there were any other tests we could do, but she again told me to try the antidepressant and call her in a month.

As I hung up the phone, I dropped to the ground in devastation. I kept thinking, "They are just going to let me die! Does anyone believe me? Does anyone know the agony I'm in?" I lay on the living room floor curled up in a ball crying like a baby. I could not stop. I shut my eyes so hard and asked God to just take me right then. I asked him to stop my pain.

After a few days, I decided that I needed to try to be okay for my kid's sake. They were going through enough right now. I could not give up. So, I tried to be optimistic. I tried to pretend I was fine.

One night I took my two oldest children to a movie. Usually when they asked me to do anything, I would tell them I was too sick. They were getting tired of hearing that even though they understood, they could not help it. I decided to surprise them with a trip to the movies. They were so excited. I was very tired and felt kind of strange, but to see them so happy made it worthwhile. As we drove home, I began to feel really weird, as if I was on a roller coaster. The faster I drove the worse it got. I could not see the road well, it felt like I was going 100 miles an hour but I was only going 45. Soon, I began to feel faint and as quickly as I could, I pulled over. After sitting for a few minutes I felt better and tried to drive again. As soon as I started driving, it started happening again. I felt as if my body could not adjust to the movement. I was terrified. I did not want to scare my kids so I just told them I was a little dizzy and needed to call someone for a ride. Well, that was enough to scare them. My oldest daughter started crying and saying they should not have let me go in the first place. I told her I had wanted to. I called my mother from a pay phone and she came to get us. We were all pretty shook up.

After this incident, I was terrified to drive. Even while riding as a passenger, I would get this roller coaster feeling. I could not fathom what was happening to me. My balance was getting really bad. I had a hard time just walking straight. Now I could not drive without feeling as if I was going to pass out. I did not know what to do. I decided to go and see my ENT doctor again.
I told my doctor of my new symptoms. Again, he was baffled. He did not know what to tell me. I told him that the doctor he had sent me to thought it was only anxiety. He disagreed. I was very discouraged at this point and he could see that. He told me not to give up, to keep fighting until I had an answer. But he offered no answers for me and did not even tell me how to get them. What was I supposed to do? I left feeling very downhearted.

By November of 1998, after one long year of suffering and searching for answers, I could not handle working anymore. I closed my day care. This decision was an awful one to make but I had no choice. I was having period's everyday where my blood pressure would drop and cause me to have to lay for hours with no strength. I had held on for a year. I tried so hard to keep my dream alive but I could not do it. I gave up. I was dying. I knew this much. I could not even keep up my house anymore and I did not even care. I could not take good care of my kids much less myself. I was feeling as if they would be better off without me. At least then they would not have to feel sorry for me anymore. Then they could move on with their life. The whole family had their lives on hold. No one knew what was going to happen from day to day. I was having these terrible spells all of the time. I thought I was having strokes or something. I would become confused and then my heart would begin to pound very hard and fast and I could not move. I would shake and my head felt as if it would explode. After five to ten minutes it would pass, leaving me weak and exhausted not to mention terrified.

I would lie in bed most of the day, forcing my body to breathe. It did not seem to naturally breathe on its own anymore. Every time I would swallow anything, even my spit, it went down the wrong way and I would have to cough to get it up. My throat seemed to be numb. My legs would tingle and go numb a lot also. Sometimes I could not even walk for periods, I couldn't seem to make my legs move the way I was telling them to. I felt like my body was going haywire and just doing its own thing. I had little control over things I took for granted before, like walking across a room or even just breathing. My headaches were always there also, but those I could handle. I had bigger problems. I felt so alone. No one could even begin to understand what I was going through. I felt like every organ in my body was not working right. I had nothing to live for. I could not even remember good times anymore. My suffering clouded everything. I could not remember how it was to feel good and as hard as I tried, I could not remember feeling joy.

Six

I felt so hopeless that it is hard to remember much about my days while I was so sick. I don't know how I made it through them. I do however remember the day I realized that what was happening to me was somehow meant to be.

I had been trying to pray but found it very hard because I felt as if my prayers were not being heard. I began to cry. I just felt so alone. Then as I was crying that incredible thing happened to me. All of the sudden, I was filled with this peaceful feeling. I stopped crying and just sat on the floor quietly, kind of looking around to see if someone was there. The room was empty except for me, yet I did not feel alone. The room was filled with this feeling of comfort. It is very hard to explain it but somehow I knew I had an angel with me. I began to talk to this unseen spirit, feeling a little silly. I closed my eyes and asked for a sign that I was not crazy. I then felt as if arms were wrapped around me. I could feel the warmth that only comes from being very close to another body. I instantly began to cry, but this time not out of sadness rather out of the joy of knowing I was not alone.

The thought that someone out there knew exactly what I was going through gave me such a feeling of relief. I asked why all of this was happening to me. I was answered instantly. It was a very intuitive communication. I somehow just knew there was a reason for all of my suffering. I was given a message. The message was that there was a good reason for everything that was happening to me and I needed to trust that there would be an end in sight soon. I was told to trust my intuition and that my story needed to be shared with others soon. What this meant was not very clear to me, but I was so relieved that I had an understanding soul with me. I did not feel as if I needed to know any more than that.

In the weeks that followed, I began a quest. My quest was to try and trust my intuition. I knew this was a very important part of the message I was given. It was in my dreams and in my thoughts constantly. When I pondered what it meant to trust myself, I felt very puzzled. Trusting my intuition was difficult when I had so much outside resistance making me feel unsure of myself.

For some reason, I began to feel this need to connect with my past. I gathered pictures of myself as a little girl. I tried to remember what I loved as a child. I loved paper dolls and Holly Hobby. I loved graham crackers dipped in milk. I loved to read and write. I made a list of the things I loved. It was very interesting to go back and think of these things that I had long forgotten about. It also felt very comforting. I decided to surround myself with anything I could find that reminded me of the little girl I use to be. I emptied a small room in my house and designated this room to be filled with things that bring me comfort, things that reminded me of my youngest years. Those years signified comfort, peace, and a love for life. In remembering all of the things I loved as a child, I realized how much of who I am in my heart has been lost through the years. I wanted to go back to who I was. Could this be part of trusting myself? Was I instinctively doing what was asked of me? I felt like I may have been on the right track, so my quest continued.

As I slowly moved about my house, searching for items of comfort, I felt a purpose. I had not felt this way in so long. I could not help but smile, for I knew I was not alone anymore. I knew I was being guided and I trusted myself to follow my intuition. It was like I suddenly was realizing that my intuition was really a channel for something bigger, a sort of communication link. Then it hit me, that is what it meant to trust myself. In trusting myself, I was also trusting God for he was working directly through me.

One of the things included in my collection of comfort things, were some greeting cards that were illustrated by Mary Engelbreit. Whenever I looked at them, I was reminded of joyful times in my past. Her artwork filled me with a joy and comfort that I cannot explain. I just really connected to her art. I began to collect as many of her prints as I could find. Included was some of her little inspirational books. I carried them in my purse.

Whenever I began to get downhearted with my illness, I would look through one of Mary's books. It was my therapy. It reminded me that there was good in life even though my own was clouded with suffering and pain. It was my reminder that my suffering would end. To me, Mary's art symbolized everything cute, comforting, and cuddly, and all of the things a little girl loves.

As I began to trust myself, which I must say was a slow process, I began to realize how much strength and power I had inside of myself. I had the ability to comfort myself during times when I was in pain. There were many times when I would be crying out of discouragement and feeling as if there was no end to the suffering I was in. As I cried, I would talk to myself, as a mother would soothingly talk to her child. I felt as if there were more than one person inside of me. The little child in me who was in pain and the strong grown up in me, always there to soothe things. I was mothering myself. This happened on a very intuitive level. Only I could know what I needed at that time, no one else seemed to understand what I was going through, so I needed to depend on myself in order to make it through the trauma.

Along with my new found trust in myself, came a determination to beat this terrible thing that was taking over my body. I knew I was not crazy. This was not all in my head like the doctors seemed to think. I had to trust my gut and it was telling me that I needed help.

Now was not a time to give up, even though that would have been the easier thing to do at this point. I was so devastatingly tired and weak, even thinking of facing another doctor made me cringe. But my mind was thinking of my children. My precious children did need me. Who could do what I did for them? Or love them as deeply as I do? No one! I had to muster the energy to keep fighting!

I saw doctor after doctor. I was diagnosed with everything from post-traumatic stress disorder to sleep deprivation. I told every doctor the same thing. I had a long list with all of my symptoms and family history. This went on for months as my health went continually downhill. I became frantic. I was suffering and obviously deteriorating and I could not find a single doctor who could help me. I became terrified that I was going to die before anyone figured out what was wrong.

Gabbi had told me on several occasions that she thought I might have Arnold Chiari Malformation like she did. I had asked every doctor I saw if this could be true. None of them thought it was worth checking into.

Besides that, I had been given a MRI right after my ear surgery and it showed nothing unusual. Still, my sister encouraged me to check into it. She never had many symptoms when she was diagnosed, but she did have severe depression and some confusion spells, both of which went away after her surgery. Neither of us knew exactly what the other symptoms of this condition were. Out of pure desperation, I decided to do some research.

I logged on to the Internet and did a search. Only one web site came up from my search. It was a site constructed by a man who had this disorder, Chip Vierow. As I browsed his site, Chip's Chiari Page, I began to have chills running up and down my whole body. I was reading his symptom list and found that I had every single symptom on the list. I sent Chip an e-mail saying that I thought I might have Arnold Chiari Malformation. I described to him what I had been going through for the past year. He wrote back to me saying that he too thought I might have this disorder. I immediately called my ENT doctor. He was the only doctor who I felt believed me that something was medically wrong. I told his nurse that I wanted another MRI done. I told her I needed it now. My ENT responded right away and scheduled me for the test. He also scheduled me for some kind of balance test called an ENG.

The next week I went in for the tests. It was an incredibly long day for me. I first did the balance test. They have you stand on a platform and attach a sort of harness to you. Then they make the platform move around trying to see if you can keep your balance. I fell over each time it moved. I could not keep my balance at all. After that test I went for the MRI. I had a very hard time with that one. I felt as if I was going to pass out during most of it. It was hard for me to lay flat on my back. That position made me feel as if my chest had bricks on it. I became very panicked during the last half-hour of the MRI. I did not know why but for some reason I was freaking out inside. My heart was pounding so fast and hard and I was terrified. Finally the test was over but I was so dizzy and shook up by then that it was hard for me to calm down.

I called my ENT the next day to see if the results had come back. He told me that I had to come in to discuss my results with him in person.

He couldn't see me until the next week. I was so upset by this. I had been waiting long enough! I wanted to know right then what was wrong with me. Making me wait another whole week seemed so cruel. I was in pain and suffering beyond belief. Even one day in my shoes was an eternity.

During that next week, I seemed to get even worse. I was dealing with the scary confusion spells several times a day now. There were many times when I would look in the mirror and not even recognize my own face. That was a scary feeling. Then there were the dreaded spells. They usually started with a burning feeling in my nose and a sulfur smell. This is how I would know that hell was about to begin. Then it would come over me like a wave of electricity washing through my body. My head would feel numb and heavy. My upper back, shoulders and neck would have this intense burning. I could not think to even formulate a sentence. I would just keep thinking the same thought over and over, "Oh God! Oh God! Oh God!" It would play through my head. I'd begin to tremble, and my heart would be pounding so hard that it felt as if it would explode. And the fear was so intense, worse than any kind of fear I had ever experienced. It was pure terror. After a few long minutes it would begin to pass, just as it came on, like a wave that was dying down. It would leave me with this exhaustion. It also left me in a state of pure panic, on guard for the next one. It was terrifying not knowing what was happening to me. I felt as if I was dying.

Besides the spells, it felt as if my body was shutting down. My breathing was getting very bad. I could not take deep enough breaths and was always feeling like I couldn't get enough air. I was still waking up several times a night not breathing. I was so afraid I would not wake up one of these times and die in my sleep. During the day, I could no longer care for my kids. I had to send them to a neighbor of mine, Diane, who I had recently become good friends with. I knew fate had brought her into my life because if it wouldn't have been for her, my kids would have suffered from neglect. I did not have it in me to take care of them. My energy was gone. Even getting out of bed hurt, my body was so tired that the slightest strain was torture. Even to talk, at times was too difficult for me.

As I went through that long week, waiting to find out if I had an answer to my mysterious illness, I prayed and prayed. I needed strength from God. I did not feel as if I could go through another week of suffering alone.

Finally, my big day was here. I was going to get my test results. I knew already in my heart what the results were, but I needed it confirmed. I had been feeling as if I was crazy for so long. Having so many doctors telling me I was fine had made me question myself. I needed validation as much as I needed relief from my symptoms.

Diane drove me to the clinic to see my ENT. When my doctor came in to talk to me, he was shaking his head as if in disbelief. I was in total suspense. I was waiting to hear if I had hope. I knew I was at my wits end and would give up if I did not get an answer that day. My doctor began talking about things on the MRI. After a few minutes, I interrupted him and asked, "Well, do I have Arnold Chiari Malformation or not?" He seemed a little taken back by my assertiveness. He looked at the films and said, "As a matter of fact, you do have a mild Chiari malformation." I started sobbing. He came to console me, but I was crying out of pure relief and joy. I had waited so long for this day. I remember my tears stopping long enough to ask my doctor if this meant I had a chance of being normal again. He hesitated to answer me. He decided to send me to Dr. Nussbaum, the head neurosurgeon at the U of M, to be evaluated.

I was so excited that I finally had hope. I was going to be treated and feel better soon. I had already decided before I saw the neurosurgeon, that I wanted my surgery as soon as possible. Yes, it was brain surgery, but I did not care. I needed relief from my symptoms and was willing to go through anything to get it.

Brett came with me to meet with Dr. Nussbaum. We were both very excited that I was finally going to be taken seriously now that I had a diagnosis. Before my appointment, I did extensive research on Arnold Chiari Malformation. I wanted to know exactly what I was talking about when I met with the surgeon. Through Chip's web site and The World's ACM Association web site on the Internet, I learned so much. I learned that in a Chiari malformation, the tail end of your brain, the cerebral tonsils, actually protrude downward into the spinal canal. Not only does this cause compression of the brain and nerves in that area, but it also causes cerebro spinal fluid blockage, which normally should be able to flow freely. The symptoms are vast because of all of the different areas involved and compressed.

My symptoms were pretty bad the day I met with the surgeon. I was very faint and weak. When Dr. Nussbaum came in to talk with us, I felt as if I was going to cry. My blood pressure was very low, which made me tearful. I could not help but be emotional. I was so exhausted from all I had been through. The doctor told us that I did have a mild Chiari malformation, but he did not feel it was causing my symptoms. My heart dropped. He explained to us that Chiari malformations did not cause the kind of symptoms that I was describing. I argued with him on that because I knew he was wrong based on the information I had found on the World's ACM web site. He seemed upset that I was challenging him. He told us that he did not feel that I was a candidate for surgery. He wanted to do further tests to see if I may have Multiple Sclerosis. The other diagnosis he suggested was that I might be having emotional difficulties. Brett and I were extremely upset. We argued with him saying that we knew Chiari was my problem. Finally, after he realized we were not going to leave until he satisfied us, he said he wanted me to have another MRI done. He told us that if a second MRI showed the Chiari malformation, he would consider treating me. This was not acceptable to me. We did not have medical insurance and could not afford another MRI. I explained this to him but he insisted he would do nothing until he saw another MRI.

We had no choice but to agree to this. In my mind, I thought of all the medical bills we already owed for my ear surgery. I had tried to get medical insurance but could not find a company who would cover me due to my preexisting conditions. I had even applied for state aid but we did not qualify. So we were on our own with the cost.

I was scheduled to have the MRI scan that afternoon. We sat in the hospital lobby for a few hours, waiting for the appointment. During those hours, I became incredibly sick. I felt nauseous and as if I could not hold myself up. I began to have clear fluid leaking from my ear again. I went into the bathroom and fell to the floor, I felt confused and afraid, something bad was happening inside of me. I could not get up, I could not do anything. I kept telling myself to get up, but my body would not listen to me. I finally was able to stumble out of the bathroom. I walked down the hall trying to reach Brett. I had to lean on the wall because I could hardly hold myself up. I did not know what was going on but I was terrified. Here I was in a hospital, where I should feel safe yet, I didn't because I knew they could not help me. It seemed they did not even think anything real was wrong with me.

I reached Brett and fell on him and began to cry. He just held me. I'm sure he was confused. I told him something bad was happening. My back and neck were burning so intensely, I could hardly stand it. I thought I was going to pass out in his arms. An older woman, who was watching this whole thing, came up to us very concerned. I could not explain to her what was happening to me since I really did not know. She could sense something though, and she began to pray for me. She told me a story of how she had been afflicted with an illness that the doctors told her she would not recover from. She explained how she prayed for healing and received it. Her calmness and gentleness towards me helped me to relax. She also reminded me to pray and that is what I did. My prayer was simple, "God, help me, God, help me." is what I prayed over and over. It was all I could think of.

During my MRI, my whole body burned and a weird sensation kept running through my body. It felt like bursts of adrenaline kept shooting through me. It was so scary. Finally it was over and we went back over to Dr. Nussbaum's clinic to discuss the results with him. He had told us to come back when we were through. When we got there, his nurse told us that he had left for the day. I was extremely discouraged as we went home.

The next day I called Dr. Nussbaum. He returned my call later and told me he still did not feel as if my mild Chiari malformation was causing my symptoms. He said he would do further tests to look for other things that could be causing my symptoms but he would not consider treating my Chiari.

I was devastated. That long miserable day of waiting and going through another MRI was wasted. Not to mention would cost me thousands of dollars! I didn't know what to do. If the head of neurosurgery at this huge medical university would not help me, who would?! I could tell I was in for the challenge of my life. Was I up for it? Not really, but I had no choice. I needed relief and I knew I needed it soon!

The only way I can think of to describe the state of mind I was in is frantic. I felt as if I was deteriorating very fast. I had so many symptoms that plagued me now, constantly. I was so afraid and felt as if it was me against the medical field. How could I win a battle like that? I had nothing but how I felt and my intuition behind me, they had all the real power, which my life depended on.

I joined the World's Arnold Chiari Malformation Internet based support group. There were about 300 members at the time. As I told my story and asked for advice, I learned that what I was going through with the doctors was very typical. In fact many members had suffered years searching for a doctor to help them. The things I shared in common with these people shocked me. I had felt so alone in this. I had no idea there were so many others going through the same nightmare. That made me feel as if I needed to fight not just for myself anymore, but for all of the others suffering who were too weak to do anything. I vowed to myself that I would do something to help others when I got better. Why didn't the doctors listen to us? Why were we pushed aside and left to suffer?

I decided to call a different neurosurgery clinic. Neurosurgery Associates was where the surgeon who treated my sisters Chiari worked. When I called, I found out that they had a neurosurgeon that specialized in Chiari malformations. I scheduled an appointment with him. I was feeling much more hopeful since this doctor, Dr. Partington, knew about my condition. I had my records transferred from the U of M to this new neurosurgery clinic.

During this appointment I was very surprised because it seemed as if Dr. Partington was interrogating me. He even challenged my honesty about my symptoms when I told him that at times one of my legs would go numb from the knee down. He told me that was anatomically impossible for that to happen. This really upset me because I was just telling him what had truly happened to me. How could he tell me I was lying, he did not live in my body? Towards the end of my appointment, I realized what was going on. Dr. Partington told me that Dr. Nussbaum, the neurosurgeon I had seen before from the U of M, had sent a letter to him prior to my appointment. It stated that my mild Chiari was not severe enough to be symptomatic and also his opinion that I was in a very emotional state. Dr. Partington told me flat out that I was going to have a really hard time finding a doctor who would go against Dr. Nussbaum's opinion since he had such respectable position as the head neurosurgeon at this well-known medical university. I became very upset by this and began to cry. I told him that I was sure that my Chiari malformation was causing my problems and was willing to take the risk of the surgery possibly not helping me.

Finally, he told me that he also felt convinced that my Chiari was causing my symptoms, but he first wanted to see my sister's MRI films to compare them with mine. Why he wanted to do this, I'm not sure. I was just relieved that he was agreeing to help me. He said he would call me at the end of the week to discuss scheduling surgery. I told him to please remember to call me because I could not take much more of the suffering. He promised me he would not forget. I left feeling like I could relax. I had finally found a doctor who would help me. He may not have treated me the nicest, but at that point I didn't really care. I was desperate for relief.

That Friday, I took a turn for the worse. Before Brett left for work that morning I told him I felt really dizzy and weird but he said he had to go to work. By mid-morning, as I sat at my computer, I began going into one of my spells. It was worse than usual this time. I called my sister. As soon as she heard my voice, she rushed over. My speech was slurred and I was not making much sense. She knew something bad was happening. My sister lives very close to me and arrived in minutes. She called the nearest hospital and told them we were coming in. On the ride to the hospital, I began to faint several times. As I would feel myself passing out, my adrenaline would shoot through my body. I knew something really bad was happening and my body kept going into panic mode. It was the most horrid feeling I had ever felt. It is indescribable how terrified I felt.

When we arrived at the hospital, an ER doctor met us immediately. He evaluated me and was very puzzled. We told him I had a Chiari malformation. He informed us that he had never heard of the disorder. He quickly made some phone calls to find out what to do for me. When he came back, he told us that he was extremely concerned that my brain was blocking my spinal flow. I was hooked up to all kinds of monitors. Every few minutes, my heart rate would suddenly increase. As it did this, I would get this burning sensation through my body and feel very confused. These episodes lasted a few minutes and each time the heart monitor would begin to show my heart racing, the doctor would get this look of panic. This terrified me. It was clear he had no idea what to do.

The ER doctor called Dr. Partington. I told him that I had seen this doctor earlier that week and was waiting for him to call me to set up my surgery. I was shocked when the ER doctor came in and told me that when he called Dr. Partington, he was told that I was not his patient and that he did not plan on treating me at all. The ER doctor told him he was going to send me by ambulance to his hospital since he was not trained enough to do anything for me. Dr. Partington told him he would not see me.

I was devastated when I heard this. I told the ER doctor that Dr. Partington had promised to call me and told me he would treat my Chiari after he looked at my sister's MRI. I could tell that the ER doctor believed me. He told me he was very worried I was going to have a total spinal blockage if I did not get help soon. He told me he did not care what Dr. Partington said he was sending me to the other hospital any ways. He felt that I was in danger.

By this time, Brett had arrived at the hospital and was told to immediately take me to the other hospital. The ER doctor called the hospital and told them I was on my way and to have a neurologist waiting for me.

When we arrived at the other hospital, I could barely walk. My legs had very little feeling in them. I felt so weak I thought I was going to collapse. We made it into the small ER room and were met by a neurologist, Dr. White. He was very angry. He asked me what I expected him to do for me. He told me that two other neurosurgeons had told me that my Chiari was not causing problems for me, why was I insisting it was? He told me that he was trying to leave for a vacation and I was holding him up. He also told me that all my symptoms could be stress related. He would not let me get a word in. He would not even listen to the reason I was there. He had called Dr. Partington before I had arrived, who informed him that he would not treat me and that Chiari was not my problem. Dr. White also asked me why I waited until late Friday afternoon to deal with this problem. He told me he was sick of people rushing in just before the weekend, screwing up doctor's plans. I had not planned on this happening on a Friday afternoon, I could not help it! When I became very upset, Dr. White changed his tone and did apologize for his anger. He told me he was not going to charge me for the ER visit and that he would not even record it. I knew he was only trying to cover his actions, not save me money. This was such a distressing experience for me. I could not even believe that this kind of thing could happen to people. I felt as if I was being kicked while I was down. As we left the hospital, I had to lean against Brett to walk. My strength was gone. I was exhausted and devastated. I was back at square one.

I was in shock at how under educated the medical field was on this disorder. Why didn't any of the doctors I saw know that leaving me untreated could cause permanent damage such as paralysis? Not to mention how a blockage of spinal fluid can cause damage of its own. After the little bit of research I had done on the brain, and Chiari malformations, and all of the related problems that can arise from compression on the brain, even I knew how serious this was, why didn't the doctors?

These questions scared me. I felt as if I knew more about my condition than the specialists I had seen did. I thought of all of the others who must feel so hopeless because of this ignorance. I was lucky enough to have the resources to find information on the Internet. What about people who rely on their doctor's knowledge and trust everything they are told? I realized that this was a problem bigger than I knew. It was not just my personal struggle anymore. I could not sit back and let this go on. I felt compelled to do something to help all of the others like me. I did not know what to do about this but I knew that I needed to get help for myself first or I would be no good for anyone.

The weekend after this ordeal was awful. My body was in a state of panic. I had the burning sensations and felt really strange mentally. I felt as if I had nowhere else to turn. I was staying with my mother now. I could not handle the slightest amount of stimulation or my body seemed to go on overload. My mind could not even handle hearing the voices of my own children. I could not function at all anymore. My family was sure they were watching me die. I could see it in their faces. Total fear engulfed us all. I will never forget the energy that filled my mother's house that weekend. It was pure hopelessness and despair, just waiting for the next spell to come. My thoughts were on my children. I was in such pain over what they were going to go through without me. I truly felt I was going to die.

A friend of mine called me that Sunday. She suggested that I call the neurosurgeon that her girlfriend worked for as a nurse. On Monday morning I called to schedule an appointment. It seemed like a shot in the dark but I decided it might well be my last hope.

Seven

Mentally, I felt as if I was in a fog. I could not see beyond my pain. It consumed me. I could not even cry anymore, my tears were stuck. Everything felt stuck. My life was like a record skipping, playing the same dreadful tune over and over. I needed a miracle so in my mind I turned everything over to God.

Brett brought me to the appointment that I secretly vowed would be my last. If I did not get help this time, I knew I would give up. As we waited to see the doctor, I laid on Brett's arm. I felt like a little girl. I was so dependent on him at this point that he did not feel like a husband anymore, more like a father. He was my comfort.

As the nurse called my name, I slowly followed her, dreading what I was about to hear. Dr. Theinprasit came in. I had brought my recent MRI's and the ones taken the year before. This doctor took one brief look at my films and turned to me and said I definitely had a problem. My spirits rose just slightly, I tried not to get my hopes up. He asked me some questions and then explained to me that my brain was very compressed and was causing all of the symptoms I was having. He told me about the surgery I would have to undergo to relieve the compression. I could not believe my ears. Finally a doctor who knew what he was talking about. I asked him how this happened and if it was really a mild malformation like I had been told. He took the time to answer all of my questions. He did a neurological exam, which indicated some dysfunction also. By the end of my appointment, I had learned that the clear fluid leaking from my ear the past couple of years was spinal fluid. This is why I felt sick and lethargic whenever I had the drainage. I learned how dangerous it was to have a spinal fluid leak and how lucky I was to be alive. My ear doctor had never noticed or paid enough attention to realize I had a leak after my ear surgery. I also was told that although I had a predisposition to the Chiari malformation, it was the trauma of my ear surgery that actually caused my brain to herniate into my spinal canal. That is why I awoke from my ear surgery in so much severe pain. It is also why my symptoms came on so suddenly after the surgery.

I told Dr. Theinprasit of the hell I had been through with all of the other doctors, he wasn't at all surprised. He told me that there were not many neurosurgeons in the area that were familiar enough with Chiari malformations to diagnose them. The doctor looked at my MRI from the year before. It had been taken right after my ear surgery when I first began complaining of my symptoms. That MRI also showed the Chiari. I asked why the radiologist did not see it and said it was normal. The doctor again said that not many people in the medical field were familiar with this condition. When I questioned him about the strange spells I had been having, I was told they were seizures. I was surprised because I thought you went unconscious with seizures. Apparently my brain was having seizures when my spinal fluid would get blocked.

I was scheduled to have brain surgery for the following week. Making it through this final week was hard. I had a lot of worries but none of them exceeded my desire to be normal and feel good again. I seemed to spend most of the week in bed. The kids were at Diane's most of the time. She was their temporary mother. I was so glad to have someone who could be there for them. Diane exceeded any requirements of a friend. She took the kids shopping and out to dinner, anything she could to ease things for them and give them what I couldn't.

Finally, it was the night before surgery. I lay in bed terrified, trying to sleep. What if's kept coming in my mind. I prayed to be able to sleep and to get me through the next day. As I awoke the next morning, I felt something on my chest. I reached down to feel what it was. It was my necklace, off my neck and clasped, lying on my heart. Instantly I knew it was my sign that I would be okay. There was no way the necklace could have fallen off of my neck, plus clasped by itself. There were two separate clasps on it. I was sure it was put there as a sign.

As I was getting ready for surgery, I noticed that Brett looked incredibly crabby. When I asked him about it he snapped at me. I knew I could not handle a fight that morning. I told Brett that I was going to ride with my sister to the hospital if he was going to be mean. He just told me to go ahead and ride with her. I knew that he was just as scared as I was, but I still took it very personal that he was treating me this way when I was about to have brain surgery.

My sister and I arrived at the hospital before Brett. I gave my sister an envelope and asked her to give it to Brett after they took me in for surgery. It was a note I had wrote for him the day before. I knew he would worry through my whole surgery and feel guilty for being mean. My note told him to say a pray and leave thing's in God's hands.

It was March 24, 1999. I was about to undergo brain surgery. I felt as if I was about to be reborn, in my heart I knew I had been living with this problem for all of my life. As I was taken down for surgery, I began to panic. Then, before I knew what hit me they put me under the anesthesia. When I woke, I did have some pain, but I was pretty out of it. When my doctor came in to talk to me he told me that I had been very compressed. More so than the MRI actually had shown. The other doctors had thought I had a mild herniation of the brain, maybe 5 millimeters, but actually it was at least a 15-millimeter herniation. My doctor told me that I definitely had needed the surgery urgently. I was incredibly relieved for it to be over! I had believed in my intuition and myself and fought so hard for help. Now I could thank God for the glimpses he gave me throughout this ordeal that kept me true to myself.

After a couple of days in the hospital, I went home, actually to my mother's. I stayed at my mom's for a week and then tried to go home. Within a day, I was back at moms. I was not ready for the commotion yet. Recovery was strange. I felt so different. Even though I had a lot of pain in my head from the surgery, I felt better than I had before surgery. I knew I was not up to doing anything at all for a while, but mentally I felt a huge relief.

After a couple months, I was back home and trying to settle into life. Most of my pre-op symptoms were gone. I felt like a different person physically but I was far from recovered. Emotionally, I felt like I was a wreck. Because of having to fight with doctors for so long, being shoved away and told nothing was wrong with me, I was traumatized. For so long I had felt as if I were going to be left to die and I was having a hard time healing from that. My trust in doctors was gone. My trust in my own body was gone. I was terrified of getting sick again. As I healed physically, I began going downhill emotionally. I felt as if deep in my mind I kept going over all that had happened the year before, trying to make some sense of it. As I did this, my mind went on overload.

I began to have panic attacks quite often. They were awful! I would panic while driving, or if I felt the slightest feeling that reminded me of my pre-operation symptoms. I panicked at everything that I thought might not be safe. Soon, I was becoming afraid to even leave my house.

I didn't understand what was happening to me. I had become afraid of everything. I was worried that maybe something else was wrong with me now. I knew I had to do the thing I dreaded most, see my doctor.

My doctor thought I might be suffering from post-traumatic stress disorder with panic attacks. I was given a medication for this. I could not make myself take the medication because I was too afraid of the side effects. I felt that anything bad that could possibly happen to me would happen to me. I knew had to beat this thing on my own.

A close friend of mine had a different theory. She thought I was reacting to Brett's anger and control. I had a hard time believing that since I felt to blame for all of Brett's moods, they were always because of me it seemed.

I began to research panic disorder and post-traumatic stress. The more I learned about it, the more I was sure that this was my problem. I needed to overcome my fears. I needed to heal from the emotionally traumatic experiences I had gone through and learn to trust myself again. But I also realized that I could not do this as long as I was in this unhealthy relationship with Brett. He kept me questioning myself constantly. The guilt kept me stuck. His moods directly affected how I felt about myself.

Then I began my book. Something deep inside of me was compelling me to write my story. I had a burning desire to somehow give hope to others going through trauma in their lives as I had. I also felt as if I had to do something to ensure that changes were made in how Chiari patients are being treated, or mistreated. I knew that public awareness was greatly needed and the first step towards understanding this misunderstood disorder. At first I thought, "Who am I to be able to make a difference?" But soon I realized that it all made sense.

My child hood dream was to write. Now here I'm faced with this great need for people to hear my story. I would have never had the confidence to just write a book before, but now, after all I had been through, after almost dying, I knew that life was too short and precious to not follow my dreams. I saw my dreams as not just unrealistic fantasies anymore, I saw them as my calling, my higher self trying to guide me to my ultimate destiny. I needed to open myself to this. I told myself, "This is YOUR life, your path, go for it!" And so I did.

As I put my story into words, I began to see a pattern. For every seemingly awful thing that had happened in my life, there was a very positive subsequent outcome. Whether it was meeting a new person who had blessed my life with a needed friendship, or changing how I saw life and myself. Each event had a chain reaction, many times with a very detailed and complex purpose with many lives being affected from one event but all in different specific ways. I began to see clearly that all the blessings in my life would not have been possible without the struggles I had been through. My outlook was changing drastically. I began to feel extremely hopeful. It was very exciting to begin realizing that everything that has happened in my life was somehow meant to be.

As time went on, I continued to write my book. I began to feel at peace. I began to trust in life again and in myself. My panic attacks became less and less frequent. I began to enjoy life and the beauty surrounding me. The most important aspect of my healing was the connection I was establishing with nature. Feeling the energy and power that every living thing possesses was essential to me, and the realization that I was a part of this was spiritually uplifting.

Meditating became my way of bonding with the spirit forces around me. Keeping that connection flowing was so important in my recovery. To me, meditating could be as simple as walking barefoot and feeling the earth beneath me, grounding me. Or just sitting outside feeling the breeze on my face and watching the tree tops sway. Very simple, yet extremely powerful, knowing that I'm a part of the utter beauty, a part of the plan.

Shortly after completing the original version of my book, I self-published it. I did not feel my book was really done but I knew so many others suffering with the Chiari battle needed hope. I published with the intent of adding more later and eventually trying to find a larger publisher to get it out there on a bigger scale than I ever could. My book was sold on a website I created and was linked with other Chiari sites. Many copies sold and I have received so many warm letters from people. I sent copies of my book to all the doctors I had seen also, hoping to enlighten them as to a patients perspective. I could see that my short term purpose was being fulfilled, but I could feel that the time was coming to face another big challenge in my life, being true to myself.

Eight

As time went on my marriage got worse. It took so much effort to combat how this impacted me. I felt like I had two forces in my life working against each other. The one trying to heal and the other keeping me stuck. It exhausted me and it was only time before I began going downhill fast. Brett seemed emotionally gone. Many days when Brett left for work I would go to the back of my closet, curl up in a ball, and cry. We had been through so much. I needed to get on with starting a normal life but with our marriage so miserable I couldn't. I tried the best I could to resolve issues with Brett but got nowhere. I felt like my spirit was going to die if I kept living this way.

As I desperately tried to hold myself together my choices became clear, either get out of the relationship or keep on sinking further. I felt like my life was at stake the day I decided to file for divorce. I was terrified at how Brett would react, knowing how he would try to guilt me and scare me into not leaving. I had seen that side of him before. I did not feel I had the strength to deal with it but out of somewhere came the courage in me to do what I needed to.

This period was such a struggle. Brett reacted as I expected and I was very afraid of him for a long time. I somehow remained strong in my decision though. I felt awful guilt over ending my marriage but at the same time knew I could not go back. My children and I went through a painful period with this, but we got through it together.

I started compiling all the poetry I had written through the years. New ones came to me at different points in time, always containing a message I needed to hear. I gave my poetry the name, The Angel Poetry Collection because I felt they were whispers from my angels to me. I have gathered the courage to share my poetry with the world. It is a very vulnerable thing to share my writings. I feel it is a part of my purpose though.

One particular poem came to me during this period that proved to be especially helpful in my healing process. It came to me in the middle of the night, as much of my poetry does. I woke up with the feeling I get when I need to write. I never know exactly what will come out of me but I've learned to recognize this feeling well. I grabbed a pen and scratch paper. I sat down at my kitchen table and wrote "Alone" at the top of my paper. This is what followed:

Time alone to honor me
to heal, to grow, to be okay
to find my way
Alone
Sorting memories
going slow
acknowledging where I've been
and therefore where I'll go
Bonding with friends
old and new
Being true to myself in all I do
Not caving in to fears
or clinging to others
or hiding my tears
Standing up on my own
Finding out who I am
Seeing that it's not so scary to live without a man
Realizing all of the healing
that still needs to come
More time alone to honor me
to heal, to grow, to be okay
to find my way
Alone

These were my instructions. I studied this poem carefully and pondered it with total trust in its message. Then I made a promise to myself to live these words until my fears subsided. Whenever I found myself regressing to behaviors contradictory to this, I pulled my poem off of my refrigerator and read it over again. It was my prayer for a long time.

My strong desire for healing and peace continued and I made the decision to begin going to classes for the Healing Arts. I completed a massage therapy class and studied energy healing. I felt a burning passion to help others heal. Through school, meditation and my own healing quest, I began to feel very in tune and trusting of my own intuitions. I learned that if my intentions were to heal someone and I made a conscious effort to have total love and compassion for another human being that a powerful healing energy could run through me into them. This phenomenon was so simple yet so amazing to me. I then began to realize, through prayer and practice, that simply loving someone without judgment at all was in itself very healing even without physical touch involved.

In 2009 I opened a small coffee shop called Earth Angels Coffee House. I had purchased a beautiful old Victorian house which my children and I lived in the upper level. The main floor and the lower level are where I operate my coffee house. Earth Angels has been a very healing place not just for me but also many others. We have healing circles there on Tuesday evenings which have been an important piece in my healing process. Meeting with other women weekly and sharing has given me the compassion and support needed to help me to face some deep shame I have lived with for years.

Finally, twelve years after the original writing of my book, I felt ready to begin writing again and tell my whole story. I opened my book and read it front to back for the first time since it published. I had been too afraid to look back and even more afraid to write about my childhood and my secret runaway years. Those things had been too painful to drudge up again. Now I knew it was time to face those things, time to heal. I began to write again, this time with no shame and nothing to hide. I remember thinking to myself, *the truth will set you free*. This time it was my truth. It has taken me several years to have the courage to share my story with the world.

As I delved into rewriting my book I began to realize that there was still one final secret I was keeping that has been the source of terrible shame for me through the years. That is my battle with bulimia. I have had periods through the years where I didn't struggle at all with the urges to purge. Then there were other times it would flare up and I could not eat without making myself throw up after. I started to see the pattern. My flare ups always came on due to relationship issues with men. Last year had been one of those bad years. I got to the point that I really needed help.

For the first time ever in my life I finally told my secret. First I told two of my children. The way they responded was so healing and comforting. I had expected them to look down on me but instead they offered so much support. They encouraged me to get help. My daughter even did research and found out where they had support groups I could go to. My shame began to melt away and I finally felt free. My urges to throw up became more controllable. I was eventually able to share my secret with the women in my healing circle. Now, I am able to freely talk about it with anyone with my head held high.

It is this part of my story that brings me to today. My book will never be complete. But all my secrets have lost their power over me now that I have released them on these pages. I began this dream of writing in first grade and now at 41 years old, I still hold this dream dear to me. It makes me really believe we are born with a destiny. Although my writings are a far cry from Dr. Seuss, I still credit his books for sparking the flame in me.

From time to time I forget the things I have learned in my life. I get downhearted and then something will happen that reminds me to be grateful for the life I have, to go easy on myself, and to embrace my beauty. I try to recapture the feeling of love and peace that surrounded me during my encounters with the spirits. Remembering I am not alone in anything helps me carry on with my own purpose here.

I am so amazed and grateful at what I've discovered in looking back upon my life. After all my years of running and trying to hide from myself, I am finally at peace with who I am. I expect life will continue to be a series of challenges and wonders, but now I have the knowledge of this healing force in me that I never knew existed before. It took me a while to realize that the prayer I wrote in my journal on May 26th, 1998 had already been answered long before. I had asked for a miracle and was shown the truth. That I am beautiful inside and out, and that is the truth about me.

www.ingramcontent.com/pod-product-compliance
Lightning Source LLC
Chambersburg PA
CBHW032011080426
42735CB00007B/566